Mirthys Melo

Artificial Neural Networks

Mirthys Melo

Artificial Neural Networks

Using Artificial Neural Networks to Model the Production of Biosurfactants by Candida Lipolytica

ScienciaScripts

Imprint

Any brand names and product names mentioned in this book are subject to trademark, brand or patent protection and are trademarks or registered trademarks of their respective holders. The use of brand names, product names, common names, trade names, product descriptions etc. even without a particular marking in this work is in no way to be construed to mean that such names may be regarded as unrestricted in respect of trademark and brand protection legislation and could thus be used by anyone.

Cover image: www.ingimage.com

This book is a translation from the original published under ISBN 978-613-9-63785-0.

Publisher:
Sciencia Scripts
is a trademark of
Dodo Books Indian Ocean Ltd. and OmniScriptum S.R.L publishing group

120 High Road, East Finchley, London, N2 9ED, United Kingdom
Str. Armeneasca 28/1, office 1, Chisinau MD-2012, Republic of Moldova, Europe
Printed at: see last page
ISBN: 978-620-7-68831-9

I dedicate this work to all Brazilians, for never giving up.

ACKNOWLEDGEMENTS

I thank God for his grace and to whom I owe all my achievements. All honour and glory to the Most High God.

To Noberto, my fellow fighter, because for those who have already given birth, there is no greater support than the certainty that their children are well looked after.

To Raquel, Rafael and Ruth, my children, for forgiving my countless absences.

To my supervisor, Professor Clarissa Daisy, an example of honesty and love for the profession.

To my course mates, Alex, Amanda, Ana Cláudia, Carlos, Gustavo, Jaceline, João, Marcelo and Romualdo, for their collaboration and friendship, and for making me believe that dreams never die

To Professor Galba, an example of dynamism, in her tireless quest to make postgraduate studies better and better.

To Professors Ana Frattini and Flávio Vasconcelos, from UNICAMP, for their support in my first academic experience outside UNICAP.

To the girls from NPCIAMB, Maria Luísa and Adamares, for collecting the data and carrying out the experimental plans, which were essential for my research.

Helena, an employee at the CCT, and Professor Ana Eliza, coordinator of the Computer Science course, for their invaluable friendship and support throughout my undergraduate degree at UNICAP.

Many thanks to everyone

SUMMARY

The success of artificial neural network (ANN) applications as an alternative modelling technique to response surface methodology (RSM) has attracted the interest of major industries such as the pharmaceutical, cosmetics, food, oil and surfactant industries, among others. Development of production media is a strategic area for the biosurfactant industry as it increases efficiency and reduces process costs. In this area, surface tension and emulsification activity determinations have been routinely used to indirectly monitor biosurfactant production. In the present work, the modelling capabilities of RNA-based methodology and response surface methodology were compared in estimating the surface tension of biosurfactant production media. The two techniques used experimental data obtained from central composite planning, with 4 axial points and 3 repetitions at the centre point, with the concentrations of ammonium sulphate and monobasic potassium phosphate as independent variables and the surface tension of 96-hour cell-free metabolic liquids from biosurfactant production media by *Candida lipolytica* UCP 988 as the response variable. The results demonstrated the superiority of the RNA-based methodology. The quadratic model obtained using MSR showed a coefficient of determination equal to 0.43 and a highly significant lack of fit. The fit of the ANN-based model to the experimental data was excellent. Simulations with the model using the training, validation and test sets showed root mean square errors (rmse) of less than 0.05 and coefficients of determination greater than 0.99. In this context, RNA-based surface tension estimation from the constituents of biosurfactant production media proved to be an effective, reliable and economical method for monitoring biosurfactant production. The work also showed the ability of the yeast *Candida lipolytica* UCP 0988 to utilise corn oil and produce biosurfactants in extremely alkaline seawater (initial pH 14), supplemented with nitrogen and phosphorus sources.

Keywords: Artificial Neural Networks, Response Surface Methodology, Biosurfactant, Surface Tension, Seawater, *Candida lipolytica*.

SUMMARY

CHAPTER 1

1.1 INTRODUCTION

Surfactants are chemical surfactant compounds that are widely used in various industrial sectors and have a wide range of applications. Most commercially available surfactants are synthesised from petroleum derivatives (NITSCHKE; PASTORE, 2002).

In the last few years of the 20th century, the world market for surfactants totalled around 94 billion a year, with demand expected to increase at a rate of 35% a year (ALBUQUERQUE; CAMPOS-TAKAKI; FILETI, 2008).

However, increased environmental concern among consumers, combined with the creation of new environmental legislation, has led to an increase in demand for natural surfactants as an alternative to existing products (NITSCHKE; PASTORE,2002).

Biosurfactants are surfactant molecules produced by microorganisms. The production of these molecules has gained considerable interest in recent times, mainly due to their high surface activity, heterogeneity and great potential for therapeutic applications, such as antimicrobial, antifungal, antiviral and antioxidant agents (SIVAPATHASEKARAN et al, 2010).

The usefulness of biosurfactants has been recognised in various industrial applications. From the manufacture of cosmetics, pharmaceuticals, food - as emulsifiers, humectants and preservatives - in the manufacture of detergents, to bioremediation applications.

Because of their diverse structure, low toxicity and biodegradability, biosurfactants have the potential to be considered substitutes for synthetic surfactants. In addition, they are ecologically safe and can be applied in waste treatment and bioremediation (PAL et al, 2009).

Despite its multiple advantages and potential for a wide range of applications, its production on an industrial scale has not yet been achieved due to the yield and high cost of the production process. One of the main approaches applied to increase yields and reduce process costs is the optimisation of production media (CAMPOS-TAKAKI et al., 2010; SIVAPATHASEKARAN et al, 2010).

The ability to search for an optimum condition with a relatively small number of experiments and the ability to interpret the effects of interactions between input variables are some of the attractive features of the response surface methodology (RSM). On the other hand, a limitation of RSM is that it generally works with linear and quadratic functions, whereas biological processes can show more complex non-linear dependencies (PAL et al, 2009). In recent decades, artificial neural networks (ANNs) have emerged as an attractive tool for modelling systems with multiple, non-linear and time-varying variables. Among the main advantages of ANNs over MSR is their ability to universally approximate functions (). ANNs can learn from historical data, without the need to choose a function to fit beforehand and still work relatively well, even with little data, as long as the data is statistically well distributed in the input domain (DESAI et *al,* 2008).In this work, an ANN-based model was developed to estimate the surface tension of cell-free metabolic liquids from biosurfactant production media by *Candida lipolytica* UCP0988. The model was trained, validated and tested with data obtained from central composite planning with the concentrations of ammonium sulphate and potassium phosphate as independent variables and surface tension as the response variable. The performance of the ANN-based estimator was compared to that of a model developed using response surface methodology.

1.2 OBJECTIVES

1.2.1 General Objective

Estimating the surface tension of biosurfactant production media by *Candida lipolytica* UCP 0988 in seawater using artificial neural networks.

1.2.2 Specific objectives

- To construct - using response surface methodology - a quadratic model to estimate the surface tension of biosurfactant production media with concentrations of ammonium sulphate and potassium phosphate as independent variables;
- To build, train, test and validate artificial neural network models for surface tension inference using initial concentrations of ammonium sulphate and potassium phosphate from the biosurfactant production media on a flask scale as variables for the network input patterns;
- Selecting the best model for estimating the surface tension of the means of production;
- Compare the performance of the quadratic model based on response surface methodology with the model based on artificial neural networks.

1.3 LITERATURE REVIEW

Traditionally, different statistical and mathematical methods have been combined to model, optimise and control bioprocesses. Artificial neural networks, fuzzy logic and genetic algorithms are examples of bio-inspired computational technologies that, alone or together, have contributed significantly to cultural changes and new advances in this area, including in biosurfactant production processes (CAMPOS-TAKAKI et al., 2010), In this work, applications in bioprocess modelling in general and biosurfactant production processes in particular are reviewed, starting from the fundamentals of bioinspired computing to neural network-based modelling of biosurfactant production media.

1.3.1 Bioprocess Modelling

Modelling bioprocesses is a challenging task. The simplest modelling concepts assume ideal mixing, which is rarely achieved. Aseptic requirements make bioreactor measurements non-trivial. Cellular processes, mass transfer and control aspects make the modelling task even more difficult. Therefore, in bioprocesses it is necessary to carefully consider what really needs to be modelled. Different tools have been developed for different modelling needs (KIRVAJU, 2006). According to Campos (2007), systems modelling can be divided into:

1.3.1.1. Phenomenological or White Box Modelling

The fundamental laws of physics and chemistry, such as conservation of mass, energy and quantity of movement, are the basis for building phenomenological models. Knowledge of the phenomena occurring in the system is based on the description or equation of these phenomena, generally derived from mass, energy and quantity of movement balances. Phenomenological modelling is limited to systems in which the laws governing their phenomena are known. This limitation makes it impossible to model the majority of systems that occur in nature.

1.3.1.2. Empirical or Black Box Modelling

Empirical modelling is normally used when there is no knowledge of the phenomena that make up the system, due to its high complexity, but there is the possibility of observing the input and output values of relevant variables during the system's temporal evolution. This type of modelling is based on techniques that seek to describe cause and effect relationships between input and output variables. In recent decades, traditional empirical modelling techniques (such as factorial planning associated with response surface methodology) and bio-inspired techniques (such as artificial neural networks) have been widely used in bioprocess modelling, standing out from traditional phenomenological modelling in terms of effectiveness, costs and development time.

1.3.1.2.1 *Modelling Based on Experimental Planning Associated with Response Surface Methodology*

The performance of bioprocesses is affected by several factors, including pH, temperature, ionic strength and concentrations of the components in the medium. Since the effects of these factors are very complex with possible interactions between several factors, they are often characterised through experimentation. To take into account the influences of the interactions of the different factors and reduce the number of experiments carried out, statistical techniques such as response surface methodology (RSM) are increasingly being used. RSM seeks to identify and optimise significant factors in order to determine which levels of the factors maximise the response (e.g. product yield or productivity). It uses statistical experimental design to develop empirical models that relate the response or dependent variable to some factors or independent variables (NAGATA; CHU, 2003).

Experimental planning is a set of tests established using scientific and statistical criteria, with the aim of determining the influence of various variables on the results of a given system or process and thus making it possible to estimate the properties of a multicomponent system from a limited number of observations. The benefits of using statistical experimental planning techniques include (BUTTON, 2005):

- Reducing the number of tests without jeopardising the quality of the information;
- Simultaneous study of several variables, separating their effects;
- Determining the reliability of the results;
- Carrying out the research in stages, in an iterative process of adding new tests;
- Selection of the variables that influence a process with a reduced number of tests;

- Representation of the process studied through mathematical expressions;

- Drawing conclusions from qualitative results.

An important objective of experimental planning is to optimise the number of trials to be carried out. This number should be adjusted in such a way as to minimise (random) experimental errors, as well as contributing to the economic and practical viability of the experiment (BUTTON, 2005).

MSR can be defined as a collection of mathematical and statistical techniques used to model and analyse problems in which the response or output variable is influenced by a large number of factors or input variables (PAIVA, 2006).

MSR is currently the most popular set of optimisation techniques. The first stage of this technique consists of modelling, which is done by fitting linear or quadratic models to experimental results obtained by means of factorial designs with or without amplification. After this stage, it is possible to move over the adjusted response surface in order to locate regions that satisfy the conditions of interest (BONA, 2008).

Some factors can hinder the survey of the response surface of a dynamic system, such as the difficulty of handling pathological or toxic agents, the collection of data points that require an *online* survey and the large number of data points collected that are necessary for a reliable result from this type of optimisation, which requires more time, a greater possibility of measurement errors and a reduction in the efficiency of the process (LIN; LIU, 2000).

However, the literature is full of studies that demonstrate the effectiveness of MSR in modelling bioprocesses (BUTTON, 2005; ALBUQUERQUE et al., 2006, PAIVA, 2006; NAJAFI et al., 2010).

1.3.1.2.2 Modelling Based on Bioinspired Computing Techniques

Obtaining a robust and sufficiently accurate mathematical model of a bioprocess is a challenging and time- and resource-consuming task due to the complexity, non-linearity and dynamics of the systems involved. Bio-inspired computational techniques such as artificial neural networks, genetic algorithms (NA et al., 2002; RONEN et al., 2002; SARKAR and MODAK, 2003, CHEN et al., 2004) and fuzzy logic (HONDA and KOBASHI, 2000), among others, have provided powerful new tools for modelling, optimising and controlling bioprocesses.

Natural computing is a multidisciplinary research field that involves new computational paradigms, based on or inspired by simplifications of mechanisms and processes present in natural phenomena, in an attempt to solve highly complex problems. It can be divided into three main areas: bioinspired computing, simulation or emulation of nature through computing and computing with natural materials. Bioinspired computing focuses on the development of tools or algorithms inspired by nature's solutions to complex problems. The simulation or emulation of nature through computing artificially creates patterns, shapes, behaviour and organisms, similar to life "as we know it", with the aim of increasing understanding of nature and computer models. Computing with natural materials mainly seeks to discover new natural materials with the potential to replace or supplement the silicon-based components of today's computers (CASTRO, 2007).

Bioinspired computing is the oldest and most studied area of natural computing. Through the creation of theoretical computational models, bioinspired computing has two main objectives: (i) to model natural phenomena in order to qualitatively and quantitatively reproduce some of their functionalities and (ii) to study highly complex natural phenomena or processes using bioinspired techniques, with the intention of solving problems that do not have a satisfactory solution using traditional techniques.

Among the most widely used bio-inspired computational techniques in bioprocess modelling are evolutionary algorithms, collective intelligence, artificial immune systems and, above all, artificial neural networks.

1.3.2 Artificial Neural Networks

1.3.2.1 Inspiration: Biological Neuron

Artificial Neural Networks (ANNs) can be defined as a massively parallel information handling system inspired by the information processing of biological neurons (LIMA, 2005). The biological neuron (Figure 1) is made up of a cell body, from which branches emerge - the dendrites - and a longer extension called the axon, whose branched terminal is called the telodendron (LIMA, 2005).

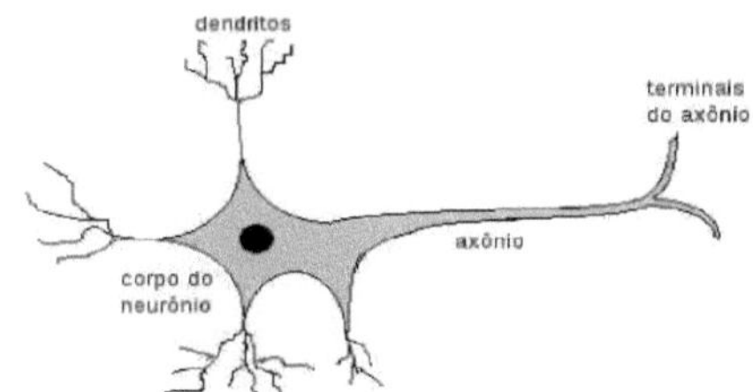

Figure 1 - Biological neuron Source: Adapted from Lima (2005)

The passage of the nerve impulse between two neurons takes place in the synapse region (Figure 2), usually formed by the union of the axons of one neuron and the dendrites of another.

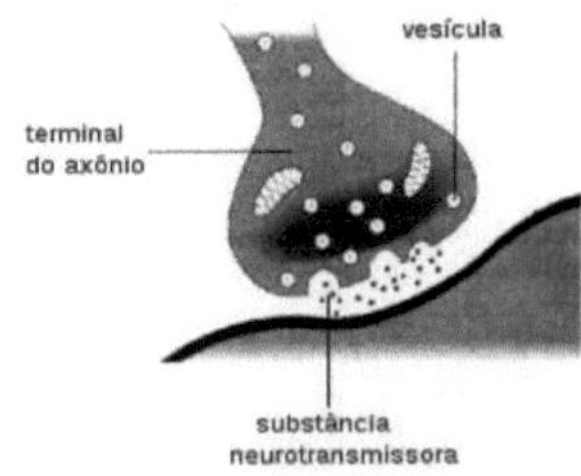

Figure 2 - Synapse of the Biological Neurone

Synapses involve the exchange of neurotransmitter substances located in the vesicles at the axon terminals. The strength of synaptic contact is determined by the amount of neurotransmitter substance in the vesicles and by an electrical threshold that must be exceeded. Otherwise, there will be no exchange of neurotransmitter substances (LIMA, 2005).

One of the most exciting discoveries in neuroscience is that synaptic efficiency can be modulated by input stimuli. This phenomenon is also considered to be the basis for learning and memory in the brain. Therefore, biological learning involves the adaptation of synaptic weights to environmental stimuli. Biological neural networks don't have their architectures altered much during the course of a lifetime. New neurons are not normally created to store new knowledge, and the number of neurons is basically fixed at birth, at least in mammals. A change in synaptic strength may be the most important factor in learning. This change can be a simple modification in the strength of a particular synapse, the formation of new synaptic connections or the elimination of pre-existing synapses. However, the way in which learning is carried out in the human brain is still not completely clear (CASTRO, 2006).

1.3.2.2 Artificial Neuron

11

The artificial neurone (Figure 3) is a model inspired by the biological neurone for processing information, based on the knowledge of neurology resulting from many years of scientific research in this area. McCulloch and Pitts (1943) presented the first and simplest artificial neuron model: the M-P model. This model became the basis for most artificial neuron and artificial neural network (ANN) models and has been applied extensively ever since (LY et *al.,* 2007).

Figure 3 - Model of an artificial neuron

Processing in an artificial neuron (M-P model) takes place as follows: the multi-valued inputs, received from other units or from external sources, are added together, taking into account the connection weights of each input. If the weighted sum of the input values is above a *threshold,* the unit's output is one, otherwise it is zero. In addition to multi-valued stimuli, artificial neurons can receive a fixed-value, unitary input, called bias, whose function is to simplify calculations in computer models (KROGH, 2008).

Inspired by the first models of sensory processing in the human brain, an ANN is a network of artificial, highly interconnected neurons, bio-inspired by the network of neurons created in the brain, developed with the aim of imitating, with numerous simplifications, the most fascinating aspect of the brain, which is its ability to learn (KROGH, 2008).

1.3.2.3 . Architecture and Topology

The topology of an ANN basically refers to the way in which the neurons are organised, in terms of quantity and how they are distributed in the layers. An ANN has at least two layers: the input layer, which receives external stimuli from the environment, and the output layer, which displays the final results of the neural network's computation. Between these two layers there can be several others, with different numbers of neurons, consisting of the way in which the neurons are structured in the network's layers. Generally speaking, ANNs can be classified according to their architecture into: non-recurrent networks and recurrent networks (Velasco 2007).

1.3.2.3.1 Non-recurring networks

Non-recurrent networks (Figure 4) are those that do not have feedback from their outputs to their inputs. They are also known as acyclic.

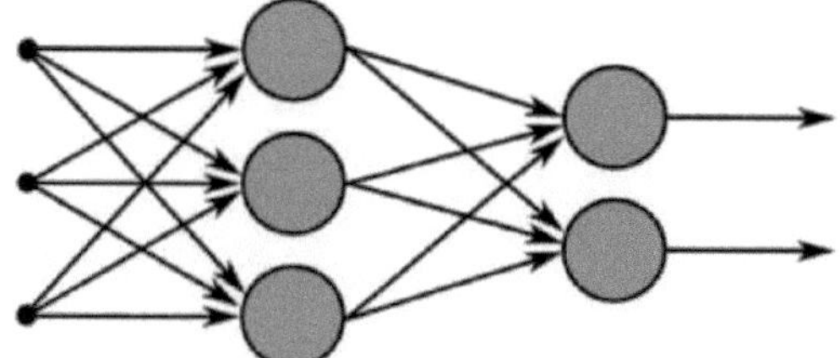

Figure 4 - Architecture of a non-recurring network
Source: Vellasco (2007)

The structure of these networks can be made up of one or several layers, each with its own set of neurons. For some authors, the input layer is not considered because it only distributes patterns. In this architecture, there are no connections linking one neuron to another, in the same layer or in a previous layer. An example of this type of architecture are feedforward networks, in which the signal is always propagated forwards, from the input to the output, i.e. they are networks whose final output has no connection to the inputs. Feedfoward networks are necessarily organised in layers and are widely used today (VELLASCO, 2007; MOZO, 2009).

1.3.2.3.2 - Recurring networks

Recurrent networks (Figure 5) are more general. They have feedback from the outputs to the inputs, and their outputs are determined by the current inputs and previous outputs, also known as cyclic networks. In addition, their structure is not necessarily organised in layers and, if it is, the networks can have interconnections between neurons in the same layer and between non-consecutive layers. This type of architecture allows networks to respond to stimuli dynamically, i.e. after applying a new input, the output is calculated and then fed back to modify the input, i.e. they are networks whose final output is linked to the inputs that behave like chain-recognising automata, where the output, which is fed back, provides the automaton's state (VELLASCO, 2007; MOZO, 2009).

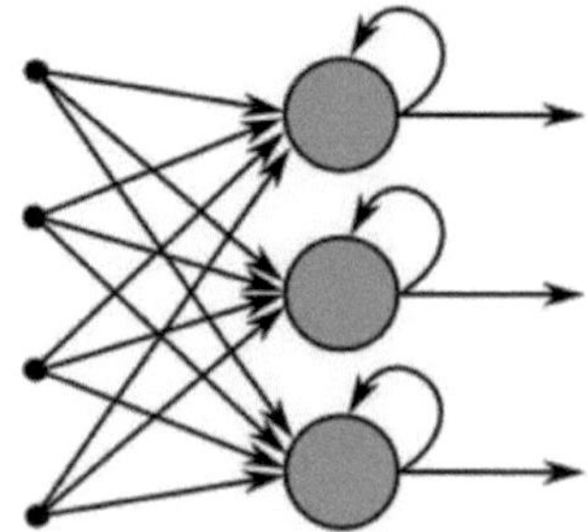
Figure 5 - Architecture of a recurrent network Source: Vellasco (2007)

1.3.2.4 . Learning Processes

In the context of neurocomputing, learning (or training) corresponds to the process by which the free parameters of the ANN are adapted (adjusted) through a mechanism of presenting environmental stimuli (inputs). The environmental or input stimuli correspond to the set of input data (or patterns) that is used to train the network. The type of learning is generally defined by the process through which the weights are adjusted (CASTRO, 2006). The two main learning processes are supervised learning and unsupervised learning (CASTRO, 2006; MOZO, 2009).

1.3.2.3.1 Supervised Learning (or with a teacher)

The learning strategy incorporates the concept of a supervisor or teacher who has knowledge about the environment in which the network is operating. This knowledge is represented in the form of a set of sample input and output patterns. Supervised learning is typically used when the output is known *a priori* and this can be used as a supervisory mechanism, as illustrated in Figure 6. The network's free parameters are adjusted by combining inputs and error signals, where the error signal is the difference between the desired output and the network's current output (CASTRO, 2006).

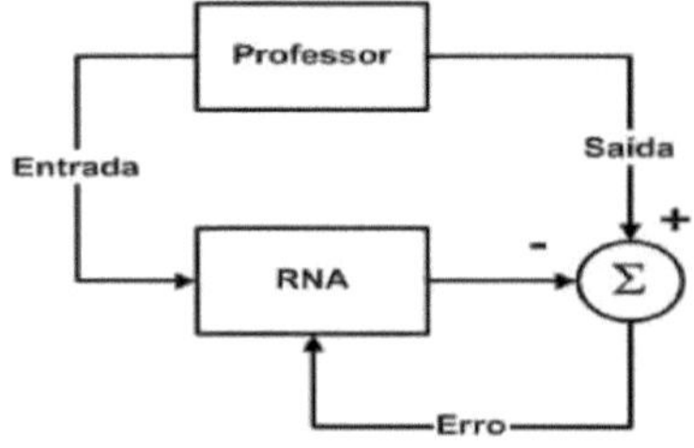

Figure 6- Supervised Learning Model
Source: Mozo (2009)

1.3.2.4.2 *Unsupervised (or teacherless) learning*

In unsupervised or self-organised learning, there is no supervisor to assess the network's performance in relation to the input data set (de Castro, 2006). *The* network has no knowledge of the output (Figure 7) and works to distinguish classes of different patterns from the data presented to the network, using learning algorithms generally based on neighbourhood and clustering concepts (MOZO, 2009).

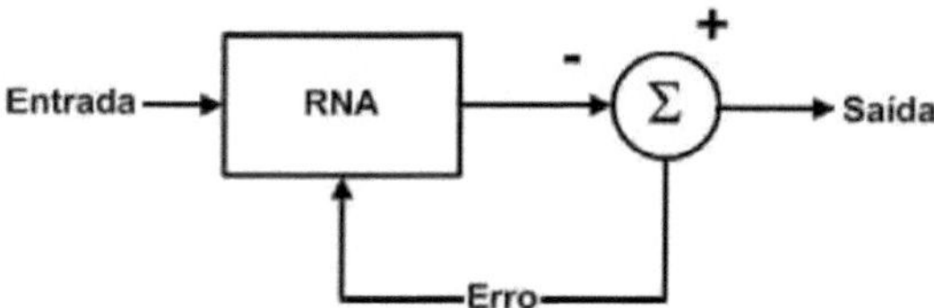

Figure 7 - Unsupervised Learning Model Source: Adapted from Mozo (2009)

Despite the similarity between supervised learning and human learning, many biological systems are based on unsupervised learning, such as the early stages of vision and hearing systems. For these algorithms, only the input patterns are available to the network, unlike supervised learning, whose training set has input and output pairs. Once the network establishes harmony with the statistical regularities of the input, it develops the ability to form internal representations to encode characteristics of the input and create new classes or groups automatically. This type of learning only becomes possible when there is redundancy in the input data. Without redundancy it would be impossible to find any patterns or characteristics in the input data (BRAGA et al., 2000).

1.3.2.5 Learning Algorithms

Learning algorithms are pre-defined procedures with the aim of adapting the weights of an ANN to fit a particular function. There is no single algorithm, but rather a set of algorithms, each with its advantages and disadvantages, differing basically in the way the weights are adjusted (MOZO, 2009).

Learning algorithms generally require a training set and the determination of a learning rate. The training set is simply a sample of data that will be used during the learning process and the learning rate is a parameter that controls the adjustments to the weights of an ANN's connections. It is important to note that the adjustments needed to adapt the behaviour of the ANN are obtained after several iterative runs of the training algorithm. With each run, the connection weights are partially adjusted, requiring several repetitions.

However, the time spent training is small in relation to the benefits obtained (CHAVEZ, 2010).

The Backpropagation algorithm is the most widespread supervised training algorithm. This algorithm, along with layered networks, has been responsible for the resurgence of research interest in the field of neurocomputing. Networks that don't have a hidden layer are only capable of solving problems that are linearly separable. The backpropagation algorithm consists of calculating the error in the network's output and backpropagating it through the network, modifying the weights to minimise the error in the next output. The central idea of this algorithm is to make modifications proportional to the gradient of the error (TORRES; MACHADO; SOUZA, 2005; VELLASCO, 2007).

Basically, the backpropagation algorithm consists of the following steps (VELLASCO, 2007):

1. Calculate the network error;

2. Back-propagate the error and modify the parameters to minimise the error of the next output.

Error backpropagation learning can be described as:

a) One step forward or spread

The input vector is applied to the network's neurons and its effect propagates through the network, layer by layer, until it finally produces the output set (the network's actual response). During this step, the network's weights are fixed.

b) A step backwards or retro-propagation

The weights are adjusted according to an error correction rule. The network's actual response is subtracted from the desired (target) response to produce an error signal. This signal is propagated backwards through the network, hence the name error backpropagation. The weights are adjusted to bring the network's response closer to the desired response (in a statistical sense).

The training objective is to minimise the average error. To do this, changes are made to the weights, pattern by pattern, of each layer, making the necessary adjustments to achieve the objective (VELLASCO, 2007).

1.3.3 Applications of RNAs in Bioprocesses

Biological processes are naturally highly complex and difficult to describe accurately by simple mathematical models. Furthermore, many biological interactions cannot be described by simple sequential algorithms or precise equations, especially when the data is complex or noisy (GAGO, 2010). ANNs have been used with great success for the design, modelling, optimisation and control of bioprocesses due to their ability to learn, filter out noisy signals and generalise information through training, validation and testing procedures. ANNs are commonly used as black box models of key variables whose relationships with other process entities are neither formally described nor mathematically established, but are assumed to occur (FRANCO-LARA et al., 2006). The following are some successful applications of ANNs, which attest to their effectiveness in modelling bioprocesses in general and biosurfactant production processes specifically.

Optimisation of the extracellular protease production process by *Pseudomona sp.* RAJR 044 was investigated by Dutta, Dutta and Banerjee (2004) using modelling based on MSR and radial basis function ANNs. A feed-forward neural network with a 3-H-1 topology, with pH, temperature and inoculum volume as input pattern variables and enzyme production as the output pattern variable was implemented and proved to be suitable for modelling the fermentation process of extracellular protease production by *Pseudomona sp.* RAJR 044. The optimal operating conditions obtained using a quadratic model developed through response surface methodology (RSM) and a non-linear RNA-based model were pH 7.6, temperature 38°C and an inoculum volume of 1.5 mL with a predicted protease activity of 58.5 U/mL in 24 hours of incubation. The normalised mean square errors obtained by the MSR and RNA-based models were equal to 0.05 and 0.1%, respectively. The results indicate a high prediction accuracy of the RNA-based model compared to the quadratic model obtained using MSR. This superiority of the ANN over the mutifactorial approach has made this estimation technique a very useful tool for monitoring and controlling bioprocesses.

The fed-batch cultivation of *Azotobacter vinelandii 21* for the production of biosurfactant was optimised by Levisauskas et al (2004). Optimisation of the kinetic profile of the feed rate and the concentrations of the components of the production medium was based on a hybrid mathematical model consisting of mass balance equations for the biomass concentration, the biosurfactant concentration, the volume of the production medium and the concentrations of phosphorus, glucose, ammonia nitrogen and phosphate. The growth rate of the emulsification activity of the metabolic liquid, as well as the consumption rates of nitrogen (ammonia) and phosphorus (phosphate) were modelled using multilayer artificial neural networks with progressive feeding, while the rates of the other biochemical transformations were modelled using specific kinetic relationships. The results revealed an increase in yield, due to optimisation, of more than 11% - compared to the initial experiments.

A hybrid model was proposed by Galvanauskas, Simutis and Levisauskas (2005) for optimising the process of surfactant production by *Azotobacter vinelandii 21* in fed-batch. Mechanistic models, engineering correlations and models based on artificial neural networks and fuzzy logic were combined to build a hybrid model, applied to the case study of the biosurfactant synthesis process. Evolutionary computation was used to determine the parameters of the ANN. The proposed model was able to represent the system's non-linearities and also showed robust behaviour.

A comparative study of the performance of MSR and ANN techniques - in analysing the enzymatic synthesis of palm oil waxes and oleic alcohol by an immobilised commercial lipase - was carried out by Basri *et al.* (2007). In this study, a feed-forward ANN with a 4-15-1 topology was implemented using the backpropagation training algorithm. The transfer function of the hidden layer was the hyperbolic tangent, and the linear function was used in the output layer. The results obtained showed the superiority of modelling using ANN over modelling using MSR. Although both models provided good quality predictions for the four independent variables (reaction time, temperature, amount of enzyme and substrate molar ratio) in terms of percentage wax ester yield, the ANN-based model showed clear superiority over the MSR-based model as a modelling technique for data sets with non-linear relationships.

An approach to parametric identification of a hybrid model based on sensitivity equations was investigated by Galvanauskas and Simutis (2007), using a hybrid model for the biosurfactant production process by *Azotobacter vinelandii 21*. The authors associated a mathematical model represented by a set of non-linear differential equations and specific reaction rate expressions with a multilayer artificial neural network with progressive feeding. The specific rate of biosurfactant production was related to the dynamics of biomass growth, and due to the complexity of its functional relationship, it was expressed through an ANN with a 4-2-1 topology, with the specific biomass growth rate and concentrations of biosurfactant, nitrogen and phosphorus as input variables. Taking into account the bias values, the ANN had 13 tunable parameters. In addition to the differential equations of the hybrid model, the corresponding sensitivity equations for training the ANN were constructed. Identification using sensitivity equations was carried out for the ANN described above.

Computer simulations were carried out using tools available in the scientific technical environment Matlab (The MathWorks, Inc.). The results suggest that the approach presented for hydrodynamic model identification for biochemical processes is robust and efficient.

The industrial production of *Bacillus thuringiensis* (Bt) biopesticides for commercial purposes is carried out through a submerged fermentation process. The cost of the components used in the industrial fermentation medium for the production of biopesticides with Bt is 45 per cent of the total cost of the raw materials used. From an economic point of view, different alternative production processes have been described as promising: solid substrate fermentation, recycling of culture supernatant and the use of effluents. In the latter case, RNA-based modelling was found to be more suitable than MSR-based modelling for modelling and optimising the fermentation medium, with different types of effluent as the culture medium for the production of Bt pesticides (MOREIRA et al., 2007).

In the biotechnological field, various applications for the use of soft sensors in process monitoring and control have also been reported (HORRMANN et al., 2008; OSÓRIO et al., 2008). However, applications of soft sensors in biosurfactant production processes are still very rare. Albuquerque, Takaki and Fileti (2008) developed an ANN-based *softsensor* for *on-line* estimation of biomass concentration in a biosurfactant production process by *Candida lipolytica UCP 988.* The neural *softsensor, with* pH and dissolved oxygen concentration as input variables and four neurons in the hidden layer, was trained, validated and tested using experimental data and showed very good predictive capacity for biomass concentration, with root mean square error (rmse) and coefficient of determination $(R2)$ values of 0.021 and 0.969 respectively. Analysis of the results indicates that the neural softsensor developed is a suitable tool for monitoring biomass in a biosurfactant production process, providing accurate *online* measurements and replacing expensive and difficult *offline* procedures.

The ability of ANNs to describe the steady-state operation of a continuous algae-bacteria photobioreactor using salicylate as a contaminant was investigated by Arranz *et al.* (2008). The authors developed a feed-forward neural network with four neurons in the hidden layer, with light, hydraulic retention time, temperature and pollutant concentration as input pattern variables and pollutant removal efficiency as the output pattern variable. The sigmoid function was used as the transfer function in both the hidden layer and the output layer. The results obtained show that the model developed was capable of accurately describing the operation of the biodegradation process studied in the steady state.

Desai *et al.* (2008) carried out work with a twofold objective: to maximise the yield of scleroglucan homopolysaccharide fermentation using empirical techniques and to compare the performance of statistical optimisation and artificial intelligence techniques. In this study, the RNA-based methodology showed better accuracy and generalisation capacity than MSR, even with a limited number of experiments. The prediction accuracy of ANNs was almost three times better than that obtained using MSR. Although MSR was useful in analysing sensitivity, ANNs were equally efficient in this respect and also showed a high degree of accuracy in finding optimum conditions and predicting the yield at the optimum point. In this way, RNA consistently performed better than MSR in all aspects.

Artificial neural networks (ANN) and response surface methodology (RSM) were used by Dasari et al (2009) to build models to describe the effects of four independent variables (moisture content, glucose concentrations, ammonium nitrate and methionine) on the yield of cephalosporin C(CPC) from *Acremonium chrysogenum* in a solid-state fermentation process. The respective applications of MSR and RNAs were found to be effective in localising optimum conditions within the range set in preliminary experiments. When the predictions given by MSR and ANNs were compared, ANNs were found to be better at describing the CPC production process. The RNA-based global optimisation routine predicted the optimum antibiotic yield as 29.4 mg/g, which is 14.8% higher than the optimum value obtained in preliminary experiments, and 9.2% higher than the value obtained using MSR associated with Box-Behnken experimental planning. The superiority of RNAs over multifactorial approaches makes this estimation technique a very useful tool for monitoring and controlling fermentation.

Rahman et al. (2009) analysed the possibility of applying artificial neural networks to predict the percentage yield of lipase-catalysed esterification between n-octyl alcohol and adipic acid to produce dioctyl adipate, using an enzyme produced by *Candida antarctica*. The variables of the neural network's input patterns were temperature, reaction time, substrate molar rate and the amount of enzyme, while the variable of the output patterns was the degree of esterification. The multilayer neural network with progressive feedforward, with seven neurons in the hidden layer, was trained using the Levenberg-Marquadt algorithm. In this study, Rahman et al. (2009) concluded that the proposed model can be used to predict the yield of adipate ester synthesis under any given conditions within the experimental range investigated.

A micro-column with pulsating bellows was used to extract bromelain from pineapple juice using reverse micelles. The micellar cationic solution was composed of the surfactant BDBAC, the solvent iso-octane and the co-solvent hexanol. Following an experimental design, perturbations were imposed on the extraction column in order to capture its dynamic behaviour and non-linearities, using the ratio between the flow rate of the light phase and the total flow rate, and the time interval between pulses. The effects of the independent variables on the purification factor and total protein yield were modelled using artificial neural networks. The best network topology obtained was defined as 16-9-2, using a moving window scheme in the time of the independent variables. The neural model obtained by Fileti, Fischer and Tambourgi (2010) using historical process data proved to be suitable for simultaneously predicting the purification factor and the process yield in total proteins. At the optimum operating point, a purification factor of 4.96 was found, with a yield of 1.29 mL/min.

Nisin is a bacteriocin approved in more than 50 countries as a natural food preservative. Placket-Burman planning, Box-Benken planning, MSR, RNAs and genetic algorithm (GA) were used by Guo et al. (2010) to model and optimise a fermentation medium for the production of nisin by. *Lactococus. lactis* subsp. *lactis* CGMCC NO. 3050. Validation experiments with the optimal solutions obtained through the association of RNA-AG and through MSR were carried out in triplicate. The average optimum concentration of nisin obtained using the RNA-AG combination was 21423 IU/mL, which was 2.13 times higher than that obtained using MSR and 8.34 times higher than that obtained without optimisation.

There are a large number of other successful applications of RNAs in bioprocesses in the literature, but in monitoring, optimising and controlling biosurfactant production processes, and more specifically in modelling and optimising biosurfactant production media, the number of published works is still quite limited.

1.3.4 Applications of RNAs in Modelling and Optimisation of Biosurfactant Production Media

Surfactants are chemical compounds that have the peculiar characteristic of possessing hydrophobic and hydrophilic characteristics in the same molecule, providing the ability to reduce surface and interfacial tension between fluid phases with different degrees of polarity, allowing them to be mixed or dispersed. This property makes it possible for surfactants to be used in industries for various functions, such as: detergency, emulsification, lubrication, foaming capacity, wetting capacity, solubilisation and dispersion of phases (NITSCHKE; PASTORE, 2002).

Biosurfactants are produced in the metabolic process of microorganisms, notably bacteria, yeasts and fungi, which have been shown to have superior properties to synthetic chemical compounds, mainly due to their biodegradability, low toxicity, effectiveness over a wide temperature, pH and salinity range and because they can be synthesised using renewable resources (SHEPHERD et al., 1995 apud ÚBEDA, 2004; DESAI; BANAT, 1997).

The major market for biosurfactants is the oil industry, where they are used in the production of oil or incorporated into the formulation of its derivatives. They also have applications in bioremediation, as a dispersant in oil spills and their derivatives. Economic factors are the main obstacles to the use of biosurfactants in direct application on an industrial scale. New technologies that make it possible to reduce production costs could make it feasible to use biosurfactants to gradually replace synthetic surfactants.

Modelling supports the analysis and simulation of a system, making it possible to create instruments capable of controlling and, where possible, optimising it. However, dynamic processes pose a challenge to modelling, as they require the capacity to process, adapt and estimate a large number of variables.

ANNs offer a great advantage for this type of modelling, as they are tools capable of creating non-linear relationships between the input and output values of a process, requiring no prior knowledge of how the process works, but only that it provides the conditions for obtaining data on the temporal evolution of relevant variables in the system under study.

The development of culture media for the fermentation of microorganisms of interest directly influences the formation and yield of bioproducts. For this reason, media planning is of great importance to the industry, as the components used in these media have a major impact on the production costs of bioprocesses. On the other hand, the activity of planning fermentation media is time-consuming and resource-intensive, as there are countless possibilities for the components of the medium and for the different combinations between them that can be tested (KENNEDY, 1993).

According to Giordano et al. (2010), a fundamental step in designing a culture medium is optimising the concentrations of its components, since the proportions of these components directly influence the amount of biomass produced and the yield of the process. The optimisation of bioprocess culture media is mainly aimed at achieving maximum cell density, increasing the yield of bioproducts and enzyme levels (DUTTA; DUTTA; BANERJEE, 2004).

There are various techniques for planning culture media. Ranging from the traditional "one-at-a-time" method to more complex statistical and mathematical methods involving experimental planning. These include: factorial planning, associated with conventional techniques such as MSR and bioinspired techniques such as ANNs, fuzzy logic and genetic algorithms (CAMPOS-TAKAKI et al., 2010, MOREIRA et al., 2007). The most commonly used method for media optimisation consists of varying one factor while keeping the other factors constant. The main problems with this approach are the need to carry out a large number of experiments and the uncertainty of actually finding the optimum conditions, as the interactions between the factors are not taken into account in this method (GIORDANO et al., 2010).

RNAs are a more accurate modelling and optimisation technique compared to MSR, because RNAs better represent the non-linearities common to bioprocesses (DUTTA; DUTTA; BANERJEE, 2004), and can be used as an automated technique for modelling, selecting and optimising microorganism culture media, especially for bioprocesses of industrial interest. However, there are very few studies published in the literature on RNA-based modelling of biosurfactant production media.

Pal and collaborators (2009) used MSR and genetic algorithms (GA) associated with RNA to optimise media for the production of biosurfactants by *Rhodococcus erythropolis* MTCC 2794. The concentrations of sucrose, yeast extract, peptone and toluene were used as input variables and the emulsification index as an output variable. The prediction and generalisation capabilities of the two techniques were compared using data from a validation set consisting of 16 experiments. The predictions of the AG-RNA-based model were more accurate and consistent than those of the MSR-based model. The AG-RNA-based model had a coefficient of determination of 0.90 and a root mean square error of 2.79, while the MSR-based model had a coefficient of determination of 0.70 and a root mean square error of 6.11.

An ANN-based model describing the relationship between the concentration of biosurfactant (output variable) and the concentrations of glucose, urea, strontium chloride and magnesium sulphate in the production medium (input variables) was developed by Sivapathasekaran et al. (2010). The model was optimised for maximum biosurfactant production using GA. The correlation coefficient between the experimental data and the data calculated by the ANN was equal to 0.9996. The average and maximum percentage errors were 0.5% and 2.2% respectively. The results obtained were more accurate than those obtained in previous studies. The optimum concentrations of the medium components predicted by the model increased biosurfactant production by *Bacillus circulans* MTCC 8281 by 70% compared to the non-optimised values.

1.4 BIBLIOGRAPHICAL REFERENCES

AHMAD, Z.; DON, M. M.; MORTAN, S.; NOOR, R. A. M. Nonlinear Process Modelling of Fructosyltransferase (Ftase) Using Bootstrap Re-sampling Neural Network Model. **Journal Bioprocess and Biosystems Engineering**, v. 33, n. 5, p. 599-606, jun. 2010.

ALBUQUERQUE, C.D.C.; FILETI, A.M.F.; CAMPOS-TAKAKI, G.M. Optimising the medium components in bioemulsifiers production by Candida lipolytica using response surface method. **Canadian Journal of Microbiology**, v. 52, n. 6, p. 575-583, 2006.

ALBUQUERQUE, C. D. C.; TAKAKI G.M.C.; FILETI, A. M. F. On-line Biomass Estimation in Biosurfactant Production Process by *Candida lipolytica* UCP 988. **Journal of Industrial Microbiology & Biotechnology**, v. 35, n. 11, p. 1425-1433, sep. 2008.

ALMEIDA, T. A.; YAMAKAMI, A.; TAKAHASHI, M. T. Artificial Immunological System for Solving the Minimum Generating Tree Problem with Fuzzy Parameters. **Revista Pesquisa Operacional**, v.27, n.1, p.131-154, jan./abr.2007.

ARRANZ, A.; BORDEL, S.; VILLAVERDE, S.; ZAMARRENO, J. M.; GUIEYSSE, B.; MUNOZ, R. Modelling Photosynthetically Oxygenated Biodegradation Processes using Artificial Neural Networks. **Journal of Hazardous Materials**, v. 155, p. 51-57, jun. 2008.

ASSIS, A. J. DE; MACIEL FILHO R. Soft Sensors Development for on-line Bioreactor State Estimation. **Journal Computers and Chemical Engineering**, v. 24, p. 10991103, jul. 2000.

BASRI, M.; ZALIHA, R. N.; RAHMAN, R. A.; EBRAHIMPOUR, A.; SALLEH, A. B.; GUNAWAN, E. R.; RAHMAN, M. B. A. Comparison of Estimation Capabilities of Response Surface Methodology (RSM) with Artificial Neural Network (ANN) in Lipase- Catalysed Synthesis of Palm-based Wax Ester. **Journal BioMed Central(BMC) Biotechnology**, v. 7, n. 53, Aug. 2007.

BASU, J. K.; BHATTACHARYYA, D.; KIM; T. H. Use of Artificial Neural Network in Pattern Recognition. **Journal Software Engineering and Its Applications**, v. 4, n. 2, Apr. 2010.

BONA, E.; BORSATO, D.; SILVA, R. S. S. F.; BENETASSO, D. L.; SOUZA, D. A. Planning and Optimisation of Mixed Systems Controlled by Qualitative and Quantitative Variables. **Revista Acta Scientiarum Technology**, Maringá, v. 24, n. 6, p. 18431850, 2002.

BRAGA, A. N.; LUDERMIR, T. B.; CARVALHO, A. C. P. L. F. **Artificial Neural Networks: Theory and Applications**. Rio de Janeiro: Livros Técnicos e Científicos. Editora S.A. (LTC), 2000.

BUTTON, S. T. **Methodology for Experimental Planning and Results Analysis.** Postgraduate Programme in Mechanical Engineering - State University of Campinas (UNICAMP), Campinas, Aug. 2005 (Handout).

CAMPOS, R. DE C. C. **Design and Construction of a pH Neutralisation Pilot Plant and Proposal of a Methodology for Incorporating Auxiliary Information into Rational Narx Identification**. Dissertation (Master's Degree in Industrial Engineering)-East Minas Gerais

University Centre, Minas Gerais, 2007.

CAMPOS-TAKAKI, G.M.; SARUBBO, L.A.; ALBUQUERQUE, C.D.C. Environmentally friendly biosurfactants produced by yeasts. Advances in Experimental Medicine and Biology , v.672, p.250-260, 2010.

CHAVEZ, A. **Artificial Neural Networks**: Workbook, 2010. Available at: <http://www.   bruce-shapiro.net/math382/Projects/content/Math382%20Project_AChavez.pdf>. Accessed on: 10 July 2010.

CHEN, L. Z.; NGUANG, S. K.; CHEN, X. D.; LI, X. M. Modelling and Optimization of fed-batch Fermentation Processes using Dynamic Neural Networks and Genetic Algorithms. **Biochemical Engineering Journal**, v. 22, p. 51-61,2004.

CASTRO, L.N. Fundamentals of Natural Computing: basics concepts, algorithms and applications. Boca Raton: Chapman & Hall/CRC, 2006.

CASTRO, L. N. DE. Fundamentals of natural computing: an overview. Physics of Life Reviews. **Journal Physics of Life Reviews**, v. 4, n. 1, p. 1-36, mar. 2007.

DASARI, V.R.R.K.; DONTHIREDDY, S.R.R.; NIKKU, M.Y.; GARAPATI, H.R. Optimisation of medium constituents for *Cephalosporin C* production using response surface methodology and artificial neural networks. J Biochem Tech v.1,n.3,p.69- 74,2009.

DESAI, J. D.; BANAT, I. M. Microbial Production of Surfactants and their Commercial Potential. **Journal Microbiology and Molecular Biology Reviews**, v. 61, n. 1, p 47-64, mar. 1997.

DESAI, K. M.; SURVASE, S. A.; SAUDAGAR, P. S.; LELE, S. S.; SINGHAL, R. S. Comparison of Artificial Neural Network (ANN) and Response Surface Methodology (RSM) in Fermentation Media Optimisation: Case Study of Fermentative Production of Scleroglucan. **Journal Biochemical Engineering Journal**, v. 41, n. 3, p. 266-273, oct. 2008.

DUTTA, J. R.; DUTTA P. K.; BANERJEE R. Optimisation of Culture Parameters for Extracellular Protease Production from a Newly Isolated *Pseudomonas* sp. using Response Surface and Artificial Neural Network Models. **Journal Process Biochemistry**, v. 39, n. 12, oct. 2004.

FILETI, A. M. F.; FISCHER, G. A.; TAMBOURGI, E. B. Neural Modelling of Bromelain Extraction by Reversed Micelles. **Journal Brazilian Archives of Biology and Technology**, Curitiba, v. 53, n. 2, p. 455-463, mar./abr. 2010.

GAGO, J.; MARTÍNEZ-NÚNEZ, L.;LANDÍN, M.; GALLEGO, P. P. Artificial neural networks as an alternative to the traditional statistical methodology in plant research. **Journal of Plant Physiology**, v. 167, p. 23-27, 2010.

GALVANAUSKAS, V.; SIMUTIS, R. Software tool for efficient hybrid model-based design of biochemical processes. **Journal World Scientific and Engineering Academy and Society International Transactions on Biology and Biomedicine,** v. 4, n. 9, p. 136-144, sep. 2007.

GALVANAUSKAS, V.; SIMUTIS, R.; LEVISAUSKAS, D. Application of evolutionary computing for hybrid model based optimization of biochemical processes. In: 6th Conference on Evolutionary Computing, Lisbon, Portugal. **Proceedings...**Wisconsin, USA: World Scientific and Engineering Academy and Society International, 2005. p. 106-110.

GIORDANO, P. C.; MARTÍNEZ, H. D.; IGLESIAS, A. A.; BECCARIA, A. J.; GOICOECHEA, H. C. Application of Response Surface Methodology and Artificial Neural Networks for Optimisation of Recombinant *Oryza Sativa* Non-symbiotic Hemoglobin 1 Production by *Escherichia coli* in Medium Containing Byproduct Glycerol. **Journal Bioresource Technology**, v. 101, n. 19, p. 7537-7544, oct. 2010.

GONZAGA, J.C.B.; MELEIRO, L.A.C; KIANG C.; MACIEL FILHO, R. ANN-based Soft-sensor for Real-time Process Monitoring and Control of an Industrial Polymerisation Process. **Journal Computers and Chemical Engineering**, v. 33, n. 1, p. 43-49, jan. 2009.

GUO,W-L;YI-BO ZHANG, Y-B; LU,J-H;JIANG,L-Y; TENG,L-R; WANG,Y; LIANG,Y. Optimisation of fermentation medium for nisin production from *Lactococcus lactis* subsp. *lactis* using response surface methodology (RSM) combined with artificial neural network-genetic algorithm (ANN-GA). African Journal of Biotechnology, v.9(38), pp. 6264-6272, 20 September, 2010.

HONDA, H.; KOBAYASHI, T. Fuzzy control of bioprocess, J. Biosci. Bioeng. v.89, n.5, p. 401-408, 2000.

HORRMANN,J.;KRALING,M.; BARTH,D.; ROCK,H. State Estimation in Biotechnological Processes Using a Software-Sensor Combining Full-Horizon Observer and Neural Networks. In: 17th World Congress.The International Federation of Automatic Control,Seoul, Korea. **Proceedings** ... July 6-11,2008.

KADLEC, P.; GABRYS, B.; STRANDT, S. Data-driven Soft Sensors in the Process Industry. **Journal Computers & Chemical Engineering**, v. 33, n. 4, p. 795-814, Apr. 2009.

KENNEDY, M. J. Review of Applications of Artificial Neural Networks in Biotechnology. In: FIRST NEW ZEALAND INTERNATIONAL TWO-STREAM CONFERENCE ON ARTIFICIAL NEURAL NETWORKS AND EXPERT SYSTEMS, 1993, New Zealand. **Proceedings...**New

Zealand, Nov. 1993, p. 252-254.

KHATAEE, A. R.; ZAREI, M.; POURHASSAN, M. Bioremediation of Malachite Green from Contaminated Water by Three Microalgae: Neural Network Modelling. **Journal Clean - Soil, Air, Water,** Germany, v. 38, n. 1, p. 96-103, 2010.

KIRVAJU, K. **Optimisation and Modeling of Bacterial Processes**. Thesis (Doctorate in Science and Technology) - Helsinki University of Technology, Espoo, Finland, 2006.

KROGH, A. What are artificial neural networks? **Journal Nature Biotechnology**, v. 26, n. 2, p. 195-197, feb. 2008.

LEVISAUSKAS, D.; GALVANAUSKAS, V. ; ZUNDA, G.; GRIGISKIS, S. Model-based optimisation of biosurfactant production in fed-batch culture *Azotobacter* vinelandii. **Biotechnology Letters**, v.26, p. 1141-1146, 2004.

LIMA, F R. **Estudo e Implementação de um Sistema de Processamento de Imagens para o Processo Industrial de Destala Mecânica de Fumo**. Dissertation (Master's Degree in Industrial Systems and Processes)-Universidade de Santa Cruz do Sul, Santa Cruz do Sul, Dec. 2005.

LIN, Z. C.; LIU Q.Y. A Neural Network-based Algorithm that Searches for the Measuring Points of a Rule Surface. **Journal IIE Transactions**, v. 32, n. 4, p. 333-343, Apr. 2000.

LY, J.; GUO, C.; SHEN, Z.; ZHAO, M.; ZHANG, Y. Summary of Artificial Neuron Model Research. In: Annual Conference of the IEEE Industrial Electronics Society (IECON), 33., 2007, Taipei, Taiwan. **Proceedings**...Nov. 2007.

McCULLOCH, W.S.; PITTS, W. A logical calculus of ideas immanent in nervous activity. **Bulletin of Mathematical Biophysics**, v.5, p.115-133, 1943.

MEDEIROS, JOSÉ SIMEÃO. **Geographic Databases and Artificial Neural Networks: Technologies to Support Territorial Management**. Thesis (Doctorate in Physical Geography)-University of São Paulo, São Paulo, July 1999.

MOREIRA, G. A.; MICHELOUD, G. A.; BECCARIA, A. J.; GOICOECHEA, H. C. Optimisation of the *Bacillus thuringiensis* var. *kurstaki* HD-1 Z-endotoxins Production by using Experimental Mixture Design and Artificial Neural Networks. **Journal Biochemical Engineering**, v. 35, n. 1, p. 48-55, jul. 2007.

MOZO, Miguel Angel León. **Optimisation of Diesel-Gas Operation in Internal Combustion Engines using Artificial Intelligence**. Dissertation (Master's in Mechanical Engineering) - Pontifical Catholic University of Rio de Janeiro, Rio de Janeiro, Apr. 2009.

NAJAFI, A.R.; RAHIMPOUR, M.R.; JAHANMIRI,A.H.; ROOSTAAZAD, R. ; ARABIAN, D.; GHOBADI, Z. Enhancing Biosurfactant Production from an Indigenous Strain of Bacillus Mycoides by Optimizing the Growth Conditions using a Response Surface Methodology. **Chemical Engineering Journal**, n. 163, p. 188-194, 2010.

NA, J.-G.; CHANG, Y.; CHUNG, B.; LIM, H. Adaptive Optimisation of Fedbatch Culture of yeast by using Genetic Algorithms. **Bioprocess Biosystem Engineering Journal**, vol. 24, p. 299-308, 2002.

NEURONIO_ARTIFICIAL.GIF. 2009. Height: 412 pixels. Width: 192 pixels. 2.68 Kb. GIF image format. Available at: <http://fu2re.files.wordpress.com/2009/06/neuro - nio_artificial.gif?w=412&h=192>. Accessed on: 01 July 2010.

NIEVOLA, J. C. Artificial Neural Networks. In: XII ESCOLA REGIONAL DE INFORMÁTICA DA SOCIEDADE BRASILEIRA DE COMPUTAÇÃO, Paraná, 2004, **Anais...**Paraná, 2004.

NITSCHKE, M.; PASTORE, G. M. Biosurfactants: Properties and Applications. **Revista Química Nova**, vol. 25, n. 5, p. 772-776, Sept./Oct. 2002.

ODMAN, P.; JOHANSEN, C. L.; OLSSON, L.; GERNAEY, K. V.; LANTZ, A. E. On-line Estimation of Biomass, Glucose and Ethanol in *Saccharomyces cerevisiae* Cultivations using In-situ Multi-wavelength Fluorescence and Software Sensors. **Journal of Biotechnology**, v. 144, n. 2, p. 102-112, oct. 2009.

OLIVEIRA, A. C. D.; SOUZA, A. A.; LACERDA, W. S.; GONÇALVES, L. R. Application of Artificial Neural Networks to Forecast Alcohol Production. **Revista Ciência e Agrotecnologia**, v. 34, n. 2, p. 279-284, mar./abr. 2010.

PAIVA, A. P. . **Response Surface Methodology and Principal Component Analysis in Manufacturing Process Optimisation with Multiple Correlated Responses**. Thesis (Doctorate in Mechanical Engineering)-Federal University of Itajubá, Itajubá, 2006.

PAL, M. P.; VAIDYA, B. K.; DESAI, K. M.; JOSHI, R. M.; NENE, S. N.; KULKARNI, B. D. Media Optimisation for Biosurfactant Production by *Rhodococcus erythropolis* MTCC 2794: Artificial Intelligence versus a Statistical Approach. **Journal of Industrial Microbiology & Biotechnology**, v. 36, n. 5, p. 747-756, mai. 2009.

POERSCH, José Marcelino. Connectionist Simulations: Modern Artificial Intelligence. **Revista Linguagem em (Dis)curso-Universidade** do Sul de Santa Catarina, Santa Catarina (UNISUL), Tubarão , v. 4, n. 2, jan./jun 2004.

RAHMAN, M. B. A.; CHAIBAKHSH, N.; BASRI, M.; SALLEH, A. B.; RAHMAN, R. N. Z. R. A. Application of Artificial Neural Network for Yield Prediction of Lipase-Catalysed Synthesis of Dioctyl Adipate. **Journal Applied Biochemistry and Biotechnology**, v. 158, n. 3, p. 722-735, sep. 2009.

ROMARIZ, A. R S. **Representation and Acquisition of Rules in Connectionist Systems**. Dissertation (Master's Degree in Electrical Engineering)-State University of Campinas, Campinas, 1995.

RONEN, M.; SHABTAI, Y; GUTERMAN, H. Optimisation of feeding profile for a fed- batch bioreactor by an evolutionary algorithm, **Journal. Biotechnology**, v.97 p. 253263, 2002.

SARKAR, D.; MODAK, J. Optimisation of fed-batch Bioreactors using Genetic Algorithms. **Chemical Engineering Science**, v. 58, p. 2283-2296, 2003.

SIVAPATHASEKARAN, C.; MUKHERJEE, S.; RAY, A.; GUPTA, A.; SEN, R. Artificial Neural Network Modelling and Genetic Algorithm Based Medium Optimization for The Improved Production of Marine Biosurfactant. **Journal Bioresource Technology**, v. 101, n. 8, p. 2884-2887, Apr. 2010.

SYNAPSE1.JPG. 2010. Height: 497 pixels. Width: 376 pixels. 71.08 Kb. JPEG image format. Available at: <http://djalmasantos.files.wordpress.com/2010/11/ sinapse1.jpg>. Accessed on: 01 July 2010.

THOMÉ, A. C. G. **Neural Networks** - A **Tool for KDD and Data Mining**. Available at: <http://equipe.nce.ufrj.br/thome/grad/nn/mat_didatico/apostila_kdd_mbi. pdf>. Accessed on: 01 Dec. 2010.

TORRES JÚNIOR, R. G.; MACHADO, M. A. S.; SOUZA, R. C. Predicting Time Series of Industrial Maintenance Failures Using Neural Networks. **Revista Engevista**, v. 7, n. 7, p. 4-18, dec. 2005.

ÚBEDA, B. T. **Estudo da Produção de Biossurfactante pela Bactéria *Kocuria rhizophila***. Dissertation (Master's Degree in Food Engineering)-State University of Campinas, Campinas, 2004.

VELLASCO, M. M. B. R. **Artificial Neural Networks**. Pontifical Catholic University of Rio de Janeiro, Rio de Janeiro, 2007 (Handout).

WERLE, L. O. **Implementation of Software Sensors in Distillation Columns with Distributed Heating**. Thesis (Doctorate in Chemical Engineering) - Federal University of Santa Catarina, Florianópolis, 2009.

YU, R. F.; CHEN, H. W.; CHENG, W. P.; HSIEH, P. H. Dosage Control of the Fenton

Process for Colour Removal of Textile Wastewater Applying ORP Monitoring and Artificial Neural Networks. **Journal Environmental Engineering**, v. 135, n. 5, p. 325-332, mai. 2009.

CHAPTER 2

Estimation of Surface Tension in a Stirred Flask Biosurfactant Production Process using Artificial Neural Networks

Mirthys Marinho do Carmo Melo

Maria Luísa Oliveira Mergulhão Freitas Henriques,

Adamares Marques da Silva,

Clarissa Daisy da Costa Albuquerque*

Environmental Sciences Research Centre, Science and Technology Centre, Catholic University de Pernambuco Rua Nunes Machado, 42, Bloco J, Térreo, Boa Vista, Recife, PE, Brazil

*Author for correspondence: Phone:+55-81-21194017 Fax:: +55-81-211940 43 e-mail:cdaisy@unicap.br

*Manuscript to be submitted to the journal Bioresource Tecnology

Summary

In recent years, bioprocess modelling based on artificial neural networks (ANN) has gained increasing acceptance worldwide. In the present work, a feed-forward ANN with a relatively simple topology (2-8-1) - with ammonium sulphate and monobasic potassium phosphate as inputs - was successfully used to estimate the surface tension of cell-free metabolic liquids from biosurfactant production media by *Candida lipolytica* UCP 0988. The results show that the proposed neural network is capable of predicting surface tension within a variation range of 5% of the experimental values. Coefficients of determination greater than 0.95 indicate the excellent fit of the model to the experimental data obtained for surface tension. The results obtained using ANN-based modelling compared favourably with those obtained using modelling based on response surface methodology (RSM).

Keywords: Artificial Neural Networks, Response Surface Methodology, Surface Tension, Biosurfactant, *Candida lipolytica.*

1. Introduction

Surfactants are surface-active agents whose main properties include their ability to reduce surface and interfacial tensions. Surface tension is defined as the free surface enthalpy per unit area and is the force that acts on the surface of a liquid leading to the minimisation of the area of that surface. Surfactants are capable of reducing the surface tension of water from 72 to 27 mN/m (Christofi and Ivshina, 2002). This ability of surfactants has contributed to their increasing application in various industrial sectors and in the bioremediation of environments contaminated by oil and oil products.

The global surfactants market reached 24.33 billion dollars in 2009, approximately 2% more than in 2008. The steady growth achieved during the period 2005-2008 was affected by the global economic recession triggered by the financial crisis. While the impact of the crisis reduced the growth of the global chemical industry, it also caused the price of crude oil, a raw material for the production of synthetic surfactants, to fall. Therefore, with the recovery of the global economy, it is expected that the market value of surfactants will grow by 2.8 per cent by 2012 (Shen 2008).

On the other hand, due to society's growing concern for the environment, interest in surfactants of microbial origin has been increasing progressively, since compared to synthetic surfactants they have greater diversity, environmental compatibility, stability to extreme variations in pH and temperature, resistance to high salt concentrations and the possibility of production from renewable sources. These characteristics allow them to be used in various industrial sectors (oil, pharmaceutical, textile and food industries, among others) and in environmental protection (Desai and Banat 1997, Banat et *al.,* 2000, Kim et al., 2000, Cameotra and Makkar, 2004, Mukherjee et al. 2006, Banat et al 2010).

From an economic point of view, biosurfactants are not yet able to compete on the world market, mainly due to the cost of production, which is 3 to 10 times higher than that of synthetic surfactants. Expanding the commercial application of biosurfactants depends on increasing the yield and reducing the cost of the process. Reducing the total cost of producing biosurfactants depends on several factors, such as: identifying and genetically improving biosurfactant-producing microorganisms, using low-cost raw materials, scaling up production and using advanced computational techniques for modelling, optimising and controlling the process. Among these factors, the use of alternative substrates is the one that most contributes to reducing costs, since the production medium represents approximately 50 per cent of the value of the final product

(Muligan and Gibbs 1993, Cameotra and Makkar 1998, Makkar and Cameotra, 1999, Banat et al. 2000, Fox and Bala 2000, Rocha et al. 2006, Albuquerque et al 2006; Campos-Takaki et al 2010, Pansiripat et al 2010).

The task of planning production media is of real interest and significance to industry (Kennedy 1992). Thus, the development of biosurfactant production media involves testing various combinations of nutrients and operating conditions, which are usually carried out using multivariate factorial planning, since univariate planning ("one factor at a time") is time-consuming and costly. The identification and optimisation of biosurfactant production media is a key factor in the development of economically competitive biosurfactant production processes (Mukherjee et al. 2006; Franzetti et al 2009).

Techniques such as response surface methodology (RSM), which include factorial design and regression analysis, are widely used in multivariate non-linear modelling to identify significant factors in order to determine which levels of independent variables or factors maximise a given response.

Multivariate factorial designs are used in this methodology to obtain empirical polynomial models, usually quadratic, relating the response variable to the factors investigated (Myers and Montgomery 1995, Nagata and Chu 2004; Desai et al, 2005). The input space of quadratic models obtained through MSR can be easily optimised using conventional gradient-based methods (Desai et al 2008). Several successful applications of modelling and optimising biosurfactant production media using quadratic models obtained from central composite factorial design data are reported in the literature (Sen 1997, Albuquerque et al 2006, Rodrigues et al 2006, Mutalik et al 2008).

However, there are several cases where polynomial models obtained through experimental planning associated with MSR face a number of limitations when dealing with highly non-linear processes. One way of overcoming these limitations is to quantify the knowledge gained from experimental trials using techniques such as artificial neural networks (ANN), which are capable of describing the non-linearities of the process. Artificial neural networks - being universal function approximators (Hornik et al. 1989) - are an excellent alternative to traditional polynomial models and for this reason they are being increasingly applied to modelling and optimising biosurfactant production methods (Albuquerque et al 2008; Pal et al 2009, Sivapathasekaran et al 2010).

Bioinspired optimisation methods have been consolidated as an alternative to gradient-based optimisation methods and have contributed to the development and increasing use of RNA in modelling and optimising production environments (Nagata and Chu, 2003; Desai et al 2006; Franco-Lara et al 2006; Desai et al 2008; Sivapthapasekaran et al 2009; Pal et al 2009).

Regardless of the methodology adopted for empirical modelling and optimisation of biosurfactant production media, experiments in stirred flasks are generally necessary, since carrying them out on larger scales implies an increase in time and costs. Experiments in stirred flask systems present at least four problems: uncontrolled pH, low oxygen transfer capacity, significant evaporation and inadequate mixing of the production medium (Kennedy and Krouse 1999). In the experimental planning of biosurfactant production processes, the determination of surface tension using high-cost tensiometers - involving procedures such as washing the cuvettes, buckling the DuNoy ring and keeping the samples at the same temperature, among others - is not only time-consuming, but can also generate instrumental errors of around 0.5 mN/m and operating errors between triplicates of around 2 mN/m. Therefore, the need to repeat one or more tests in an experimental design, due to error or accident, means wasting time and material and consequently increasing the cost of the process. In these cases, the existence of a reliable empirical model based on neural networks, obtained from the other tests in the experimental plan, can save a lot of time and material.

The aim of this study was to develop a model based on multilayer *Perceptron* artificial neural networks capable of estimating, on a flask scale, the surface tension of biosurfactant production media by *Candida lipolytica* in seawater - extremely alkaline (initial pH 14), supplemented with nitrogen (ammonium sulphate) and phosphorus (monobasic potassium phosphate) sources - using corn oil as the sole carbon source.

2. Materials and Methods

2.1. Biosurfactant Production Process on a Flask Scale

2.1.1. Microorganism and Preservation Medium

The yeast *Candida lipolytica* UCP 988 was obtained from the culture bank of the Environmental Sciences Research Centre at the Catholic University of Pernambuco. The *yeast* colonies were kept at 4° C in test tubes with an inclined YMA *(Yeast Mould Agar)* medium containing 3 g/L of yeast extract, 3 g/L of malt extract, 10 g/L of D-glucose, 5 g/L of tryptone and 15 g/L of agar. The pH was adjusted to 5.0 with HCl. Transfers using aseptic techniques were carried out monthly onto agar plates to ensure cell viability.

2.1.2. Sea water

The seawater used to dissolve the components of the media used to produce biosurfactants by *C.lipolytica* was collected from Bairro Novo beach in Olinda, Pernambuco, and after filtration to remove suspended solids, it had a salinity of 36%o, a specific gravity of 1026 kg m^{-3} , a pH of 7 and a surface tension of 71.34 mN/m.

2.1.3. Two-factor central composite planning

Central composite planning consisting of 11 trials, including 4 axial points and 3 repetitions at the central point, was carried out to investigate the influence of the concentrations of ammonium sulphate and monobasic potassium phosphate on the surface tension of the biosurfactant production media and to serve as a database for modelling the process. All the planning tests were carried out in triplicate. The ranges and levels of the components (factors or independent variables) studied are shown in Table 1 and were specified on the basis of a complete factorial design 2^4 (Table 2), previously carried out (Henriques et al, 2010). The surface tension (response variable) was determined in various combinations of the media constituents (Table 1) using corn oil (5% v/v) as the carbon source. The pH of each medium was adjusted to 14. The media was inoculated in a laminar flow chamber at a rate of 5% of the media volume, using a suspension of 10^7 *Candida lipolytica* cells per mL of sterile seawater. The 1000 mL Erlenmeyer flasks with a useful volume of 750 mL were incubated on a rotary shaker at 28° C and 150 rpm for 96 hours. Determinations of biomass concentration and pH, salinity, specific gravity, emulsification activity and surface tension. of the cell-free cultures were carried out at 0 and 96 hours.

1.1.1. Analytical Methods

The biomass concentration (dry mass) was determined by gravimetry, by filtering the culture medium through a 0.22 Dm Milipore membrane, drying it at 70° C until it was dry and weighing it on an analytical balance. Hydrogen potentials were determined by potentiometry. Salinities and densities (specific gravities) were determined using a handheld refractometer without automatic temperature compensation, with a scale between 0 and 100%o (ppt) salinity and 1000 to 1070 specific gravity, resolution 0.7%o. The emulsification activity for water-in-hexadecane emulsion was determined according to the method described by Cirigliano and Carman (1984). The method defines an emulsification unit as the amount of emulsifier that produces an emulsion with an absorbance of 1.0 at 540 nm, i.e. the amount of emulsifier capable of raising the absorbance of the system by one unit. Surface tensions were determined using the *Du Noy* ring method (KIM et al., 2000), using a SIGMA 70 digital tensiometer (KSV Instruments Ltd., Helsinki, Finland) at room temperature (25°C).

2.2. Modelling Means of Production based on Response Surface Methodology

Response surface methodology consists of a group of mathematical and statistical techniques based on fitting models to data obtained through experimental design. Response surface methodology associated with central composite planning was used to build an empirical model (Khury and Cornell, 1996). The experimental data obtained in the central composite planning of the optimisation strategy mentioned above was adjusted by regression analysis to the following quadratic polynomial:

$$y = b_0 + \sum_{i=1}^{2} b_i x_i^i + \sum_{i=1}^{2} \sum_{j=1}^{2} b_{ij} x_i x_j + e \tag{1}$$

where y represents the response variable (surface tension) , x_i and x_j the independent variables (concentrations of ammonium sulphate and potassium phosphate), the terms b_0 , b_i and b_{ij} are the regression coefficients and e is a random error component.

The mathematical model obtained after fitting the function to the data may sometimes not satisfactorily describe the experimental domain studied. The most reliable way to assess the quality of the fitted model is to apply analysis of variance (ANOVA). The central idea of ANOVA is to compare the variation due to the treatment (change in the combinations of variable levels) with the variation due to random errors inherent in the response measurements generated. From this comparison, it is possible to assess the significance of the regression used to predict the response variables, considering the sources of experimental variance (Vieira and Hofmann, 1989; Bezerra et al, 2008).

Analysis of variance, determination of regression coefficients, Pareto diagrams and surface graphs were carried out using the Statistica® programme version 8.0 (Statsoft.Inc, Tulsa/OK,USA).

2.3. Modelling Means of Production based on Artificial Neural Networks

2.3.1. Database construction

The database for modelling the production media (Table 3) was made up of data on the concentrations of ammonium sulphate and potassium monobasic phosphate and the surface tension of metabolic liquids at 96 hours, free of cells, obtained from trials carried out in triplicate, in central composite planning carried out as part of a sequential strategy for optimising the biosurfactant production process on a flask scale. The set formed by the variables ammonium sulphate and monobasic potassium phosphate concentrations was considered the standard input. The set formed by the surface tension variable was considered an output standard.

2.3.2 Pre-processing and expanding the database

The availability of a sufficiently large and representative database on the region of interest usually ensures good generalisation properties for the trained network. However, from a practical point of view, in terms of human (labour) and economic (capital) resource constraints, it is not always possible to carry out as many experiments as are necessary to obtain enough data to train neural networks so that they generalise well (Tholudur et al, 2000). Therefore, the original database (Table 3) was statistically treated to eliminate possible extreme values *(outliers)* and expanded to 110 patterns; by adding random noise - of different magnitudes and distributions - to the input patterns (formed by the ammonium sulphate and monobasic potassium phosphate concentrations, pH and salinity variables) and output patterns (formed by the surface tension variable). Random noise lower than the experimental errors obtained at the centre points of the central composite planning was added to the surface tension values. However, as the experimental errors for the concentrations of ammonium sulphate and potassium phosphate monobasic were (practically) equal to zero, random values of less than 10^{-4} were added to these variables to avoid problems during training due to the presentation of equal inputs with different outputs.

2.3.3. Database division

After pre-processing, the database was divided into three sets: a training set to determine the model's coefficients; a validation set to specify the model's structure; and a test set to determine the model's performance. The number of patterns in the training, validation and test sets were specified as 60, 20 and 20 per cent respectively of the number of patterns in the database. The patterns in each set were chosen at random, but care was taken to ensure that the values of the patterns in the validation and test sets did not extrapolate the values of the patterns in the training set.

2.3.4. Specification of the model structure

Multilayer *Perceptron* neural networks with progressive feedforward were used to build a predictive model, with the concentration of ammonium sulphate and the concentration of monobasic potassium phosphate as inputs and surface tension as the output. The number of neurons in the hidden layer was varied from 1 to 20. Different activation functions (linear, logistic sigmoid and hyperbolic tangent) were tested for the hidden and output layers

2.3.5. Normalisation of the model's input and output patterns.

The input and output patterns were normalised, within a range of 0 to 1, to make it easier to compute the data and use the different activation functions (linear, logistic sigmoid and hyperbolic tangent). Subsequently, the values were denormalised to allow comparison of the experimental output values with those calculated by the network.

2.3.6. Model training, validation and testing

Supervised training of a network is an iterative process in which a pre-specified error function is minimised by adjusting the weights appropriately. Once the topology of the neural network has been selected, the weights of the connections are determined. Determining these weights allows the network to learn information about the system being modelled. The back propagation algorithm (Rummelhart et al , 1986) can be very slow due to the small learning rates that have to be used for stable convergence. There are various algorithms to improve the rate and stability of the back propagation algorithm (Beale et al 2010). The back propagation algorithms with variable learning rate (Magoulas et al, 1999), resilient (Riedmiller and Braun

2006) and based on Levenberg-Marquadt (Levenberg, 1944; Marquardt 1963; Gil et al 1981) were compared in terms of their performance during training. To ensure that each network was trained independently, random weights were used to initialise each network. To avoid overfitting the model, the appropriate number of neurons in the hidden layer was determined using the cross-validation technique (Bishop, 1995; Haykin, 2001, Setiono 2001). The neural network toolbox of the scientific technical environment Matlab version 7.0 (the Mathworks Mass., USA) was used to develop, train, validate and test the neural networks.

2.3.7. Selecting the best model

With the data sets divided, models were built and performance comparisons in terms of the root mean square error *(rmsse)* and the coefficient of determination were made using the validation set. The decision on the best model was made in favour of the topology that, using the validation set, showed the greatest predictive capacity, with the lowest number of neurons in the hidden layer (Albuquerque , 2006; Albuquerque et al., 2008).

3. Results and Discussion

3.1. Modelling Biosurfactant Production Based on Response Surface Methodology

The decoded matrix and the results obtained from the central composite planning for the surface tension of the metabolic liquids at 96 hours cell-free is shown in Table 3, which was also used to create an extended database for the modelling based on artificial neural networks.

The results obtained for surface tension indicate that the yeast *C. lipolytica* UCP 0988 is capable of producing biosurfactant, at 28°C, in different media supplemented with ammonium sulphate and potassium phosphate, adjusted to initial pH 14, with seawater as the only diluent and 5% corn oil as the only carbon source. Among the various production media investigated, the medium composed of 3.975 g/L of ammonium sulphate and 12g/L of monobasic potassium phosphate (trial 5) showed cell-free metabolic liquids with a surface tension equal to 33.85±1.00 mN/m. This is an excellent result, as it was obtained under conditions of high salinity (initial salinity of the medium equal to *58%) and* extreme pH (initial pH of the medium equal to

14). However, there are no reports in the literature with similar results under the same conditions.

Work using other microorganisms under conditions of high salinity and temperature and with pH close to neutrality has also confirmed the importance of pH and salinity on the production of biosurfactants. The bacterium *Baccilus mycoides* isolated from an Iranian oil field showed a maximum reduction in surface tension (34 mN/m) under optimum conditions of 16.55 g/L glucose, a total salt concentration of 55.05 g/L, a temperature of 39.03°C and a pH of 7.37 (Najafi et al 2010). On the other hand, the bacterium *Paeni-baccilus alvei,* also isolated from an Iranian oil field, was able to produce biosurfactant and reduce the tension to 35 mN/m in an optimised medium containing 13.3 g/L of glucose, with a total salt concentration of 39 g/L at a temperature of 34.76°C and a pH of 6.89 (Najafi et al 2011). In these last two studies, MSR-based models were developed to estimate surface tension as a function of temperature, pH, salinity and glucose concentration. Both models showed no lack of fit to the quadratic model and the correlation between the observed and predicted values was high (coefficients of determination R^2 greater than 0.96).

Under the conditions studied in this study, the estimates of the effects of the concentrations of ammonium sulphate and monobasic potassium phosphate on the surface tension of cell-free metabolic liquids at 96 hours, with an initial pH of 14, can be assessed, with a 95% confidence level, using the Pareto diagram shown in Figure 1. The magnitude of each effect is represented by the horizontal columns and the dashed line across the columns - corresponding to a p-value of 0.05 - indicates the point at which the estimated effects are statistically significant. As can be seen in the diagram, under the conditions studied, only the linear contribution of the potassium phosphate concentration had a significant negative effect on the increase in surface tension, consequently favouring a reduction in surface tension. On the other hand, the quadratic contribution of potassium phosphate concentration and the interaction between potassium phosphate concentration and ammonium sulphate concentration had significant positive effects on the increase in surface tension.

In this work, a second-order polynomial model (Eq. 2) was used to describe the relationship between the concentrations of ammonium sulphate (x_1) and monobasic potassium phosphate (x_2) and the surface tension of the metabolic liquids (y) obtained at 96 hours.

$$y = 36{,}10 + 0{,}05x_1 - 0{,}40x_1^2 - 0{,}80x_2 + 1{,}01x_2^2 + 0{,}60x_1x_2 \tag{2}$$

The quality of the quadratic model was assessed by ANOVA (Table 4). The model showed a coefficient of determination (R^2) equal to 0.43, indicating a low correlation between the observed and predicted values, i.e. only 43% of the response variability can be explained by the model. The F test for the model shows that the calculated F (F_c = 0.76) is lower than the tabulated F (F_t (0.05; 10; 9) = 5.05), demonstrating the model's lack of significance and that it cannot therefore be used for predictive purposes. The F test for lack of fit was significant (p=0.009), with the calculated F (F=108.564) higher than the tabulated F (F=19.16). As can be seen in Figure 2, the experimental data does not fit well with the saddle-shaped response surface, in which the surface tension shows its lowest values around 34 mN/m. These results suggest the existence of a more complex non-linear relationship than the quadratic one between surface tension (dependent variable) and the concentrations of ammonium sulphate and potassium monobasic (independent variables) in the search region investigated. Therefore, in order to improve the fit of the quadratic model to the experimental data, it would be advisable to shift (narrow) the boundaries of the search space towards the optimum point of the process (i.e. towards the lower axial point of the ammonium sulphate concentration of the process and the centre point of the monobasic potassium phosphate concentration) and carry out a new central composite planning, which would imply an increase in time and costs. In this case, artificial neural networks, which are universal function approximators, are, as will be shown below, a faster and more economical alternative for modelling this region of the biosurfactant production process by *C.lipolytica UCP* 0988.

3.2. Modelling Biosurfactant Production Based on Artificial Neural Networks

Artificial neural networks, with the concentrations of ammonium sulphate and monobasic potassium phosphate as standard input variables, were modelled to estimate the surface tension of the metabolic liquid with 96 hours of biosurfactant production media by *Candida lipolytica* UCP 0988. Using the training set, networks with a number of hidden neurons ranging from 1 to 20, initialised with random initial weights, were trained, with different activation functions (linear, logistic sigmoid and hyperbolic tangent) in the hidden and output layers and with different training algorithms (back propagation algorithms with variable learning rate, resilient and Levenberg-Marquadt based) and compared for performance using the validation and test sets.

The networks that performed best during training are shown in Table 5. The network - with eight neurons in the hidden layer (Table 5) - trained with the resilient back propagation algorithm (rmse=0.0436, R^2 =0.9969), with the logistic sigmoid and hyperbolic tangent functions, respectively, in the hidden and output layers - was also the best performing in simulations carried out using the complete data from the validation (rmse=0.0387 R^2 =0.9960) (Table 6) and test (rmse=0.0458, R^2 =0.9953) sets (Table 7). When simulated using only data from the 11 central composite planning trials (Table 3), data that was part of the extended test set and had also not been used in training or validation, the network with eight neurons in the hidden layer showed *rmse* equal to 0.0424 and R^2 equal to 0.9980, which shows that the generalisation capacity of the selected network is excellent.

Figures 3, 5 and 7 show parity graphs, where the surface tensions calculated by the network with 8 neurons using the training, validation and test sets are compared with the corresponding experimental data. The neural network with a 2-8-1 topology, as well as fitting well to the data from the training set (Figure 4), also provides surface tension predictions using the data from the validation (Figure 6) and test (Figure 8) sets that are very close to those measured experimentally. Figures 9 and 10 show the network's predictive capacity when tested with the 11 original patterns from the central composite planning (Table 3). Figure 11 shows the surface tension values measured experimentally and calculated by the network using the training, validation and test sets, demonstrating the model's ability to reproduce the overall behaviour of the surface tension observed in the process (over 98% of the data contains relative deviations between the measured and calculated values of less than 5% for surface tension). To sum up, the results obtained show that models based on artificial neural networks are capable of successfully modelling key variables in biosurfactant production processes in highly non-linear regions, where quadratic models obtained using response surface methodology show a great lack of fit with the experimental data. In other words, in this study, models based on artificial neural networks proved to have greater precision and better predictive capacity than quadratic models based on MSR, and could be used to estimate the surface tension of biosurfactant production media on a flask scale.

Studies published in the literature - making comparisons between optimisation using quadratic models and MSR and optimisation using ANN-based models and GA (Nagata and Chu, 2003; Dutta et al., 2004; Desai et al., 2005; Desai et al., 2006; Franco-Lara et al., 2006; Desai et al., 2008, Pal et al. 2009; Sivapathasekaran et *al.* (2010)) - have confirmed the effectiveness and growing importance of ANNs as alternative models to polynomials obtained by regression. Most of these studies make comparisons in optimal regions, in which both ANN-based models and quadratic models show a good fit to experimental data. However, in practice, whether for technical or economic reasons, most bioprocesses do not work in optimal regions, but in regions close to them, which makes it important to develop models that describe such regions efficiently and reliably.

Conclusion

Modelling based on artificial neural networks has proved to be a more efficient and economical tool than modelling based on response surface methodology for estimating the surface tension of biosurfactant production media, and can be applied to other state variables and bioprocesses both to explore and expand knowledge about highly non-linear regions of the process, and to build models for optimisation using bio-inspired techniques.

Thank you

The authors would like to thank PROCAD-CAPES and the Catholic University of Pernambuco for their financial support.

Bibliographical references

Albuquerque CDC, Fileti AMF, Campos-Takaki GM (2006) Optmizing the medium components in bioemulsifiers production by *candida lipolytica* with response surface method. *Can. J. Microbiol.* **52** : 575-583.

Albuquerque CDC, Fileti AMF, Campos-Takaki GM (2008). On-line Biomass Estimation in Biosurfactant Production Process by *Candida lipolytica* UCP 988. *J. Ind. Microbiol. Biotech.* v. **35**:11:1425-1433.

Banat IM, Makkar RS, Cameotra SS (2000) Potential commercial application of microbial surfactants. *Appl. Biotechnol.* **53**: 495-508.

Banat IM, Franzetti A, Gandolfi I, Bestetti G, Martinotti MG, Fracchia L, Smyth TJ, Roger MR (2010) Microbial biosurfactants production, applications and future potential. *Appl. Biotechnol.* **87**: 427-444.

Beale MH, Hagan MT, Howard BD(2010) Neural network toolbox 7 user's guide. *Mathworks.*

Bezerra MA, Santelli RE, Oliveira EP, Villar LS, Escaleira LA (2008) Response surface methodology (rsm) as a tool for optimisation in analytical chemistry. *Talanta.* **76** : 965-977.

Bishop CM (1995) Neural networks for pattern recognition. Oxford University Press.

Cameotra SS, Makkar RS (1998) Synthesis of biosurfactants in extreme conditions. *Appl. Microbiol. Biotechnol.* **50**: 520-529.

Cameotra SS, Makkar RS (2004) Recent applications of biosurfactants as biological and immunological molecules. *Curr. Opin. Microbiol.* **7**: 262-266.

Campos-Takaki, G, Sarubbo LA, Albuquerque CDC (2010) Environmentally friendly biosurfactants produced by yeasts. *Adv. Exp. Med. Biol.* **672**: 250-260.

Choudhari S, Singhal R (2008) Media optimization for the production of b-carotene by *blakeslea trispora:* a statistical approach. *Bioresour. Technol.* **99**: 722-730.

Christofi N, Ivshina IB (2002) Microbial surfactants and their use in field studies of soil remediation. *J. Appl.*

Microbiol. **93**: 915-929.

Crolla A, Kennedy KJ (2001) Optimisation of citric acid production from candida lipolytica y 1095 using n-paraffin. *J. Biotechnol.* **89**: 27-40.

Desai JD, Banat IM (1997) Microbial production of surfactants and their commercial potential. *Microbiol. Mol. Biol. Rev.* **61**: 47-64.

Ferreira EC, Azevedo SF (2006) Modelling, monitoring and control of biological reactors. *Lidel :* 193-230.

Fontes GC, Amaral PFF, Nele M, Coelho MAZ (2010) Factorial design to optimise biosurfactant production by yarrowia lipolytica. *J. Biomed Biotechnol.* **2010**: 8 p.

Fox SL, Bala GA (2000) Production of surfactant from bacillus subtilis atcc 21332 using potato substrates. *Bioresour. Technol.* **75**: 235-240.

Franzetti A, Caredda P, La Colla P, Pintus M, Tamburini, E, Papacchini M, Bestetti G (2009) Cultural factors affecting biosurfactant production by *gordonia sp.* bs29. Int. *Biodet. Biodegrad.* **63**: 943-947.

Gill PR, Murray W, Wright MH (1981) The Levenberg-Marquardt method. *Academic Press:* 136-137.

Haykin S (2001) *Neural networks: principles and practice.* Bookman: 900 p.

Henriques MLOMF, Silva AM, Antunes AA, Jara AMAT, Campos-Takaki G.M, Albuquerque CDC Production of Bioemulsifier/Biosurfactant in Seawater under Extreme pH Conditions. In: XX Latin American Congress of Microbiology, Montevideo, Uruguay. 27-30 Sep 2010.

Khuri AI, Cornell JA (1996) Response surfaces: designs and analysis. *Marcel Dekker.*

Kennedy M (1992) Designing fermentation media: a comparison of neural networks to factorial design. *Biotechnol Tech.* **6**(4): 293-298.

Kennedy M, Krouse D (1999) Strategies for improving fermentation medium performance: a review. *J. Ind. Microbiol. & Biotechnol.* **23**: 456-475.

Kim SH, Lim EJ, Lee SO, Lee JD, Lee TH (2000) Purification and characterisation of biosurfactants from nocardia sp. l - 417. *Biotechnol. Appl. Biochem* **31**: 249-253.

Levenberg K (1944) A method for the solution of certain non-linear problems in least squares. *Quarterly Appl. Math.* **2**: 164-168.

Magoulas GD, Vrahatis MN, Androulakis GS (1999) Improving the convergence of the backpropagation algorithm using learning rate adaptation methods. *Neural Comput.* **11**: 1769-1796.

Makkar RS, Cameotra SS (1999) Biosurfactant production by microorganisms on unconventional carbon sources - a review. *J. Surfact. Detergent.* **2**: 237-241.

Marquardt DW (1963) Algorithm for the least-squares estimation of nonlinear parameters. *J. Indust. Appl Math.* **11**: 431-441 .

Mukherjee S, Das P, Sen R (2006) Towards commercial production of microbial surfactants. *Trends Biotechnol.* **24**: 509-515.

Mulligan CN, Gibbs BF (1993) Factors influencing the economics of biosurfactants. *Marcel Decker:* 392371.

Mulligan CN, Yong RN, Gibbs BF (2001) Surfactant-enhanced remediation of contaminated soil: a review. *Eng. Geol.* **60**: 371.

Mutalika SR, Vaidyaa BK, Joshia RM, Desai KM, Nene SN (2008) Use of response surface optimisation for the production of biosurfactant from *rhodococcus* spp. mtcc 2574. *Bioresour. Technol.* **99**: 7875-7880.

Myers RH, Montgomery DC, Anderson-cook CM (1995) Response surface methodology: process and production optimisation using designed experiments. *Wiley.*

Nagata Y, Chu HK (2003) Optimisation of a fermentation medium using neural networks and genetic algorithms. *Biotech. Lettrs.* **25**: 1837-1842.

Pansiripat S, Pornsunthorntawee O, Rujiravanit R, Kitiyanan B, Somboonthanate P, Chavadej S (2010) Biosurfactant production bypseudomonas *aeruginosa* sp4 using sequencing batchreactors: effect of oil-to-glucose ratio. *Biochem. Eng. J.* **49**: 185-191.

Rocha MVP, Oliveira AHS, Souza MCM, Gonçalves LRB (2006) Natural cashew apple juice as fermentation medium for biosurfactant production by acinetobacter calcoaceticus. *World J. Microbiol. Biotechnol.* **22**: 1295-1299.

Rodrigues L, Teixeira J, Oliveira R, Van der mei HC (2006) Response surface optimisation of the medium components for the production of biosurfactants by probiotic bacteria. *Process. Biochem.* **41**: 1-10.

Sen R (1997) Response surface optimization of the critical media components for the production of surfactin. *J. Chem. Technol. Biotechnol.* **68**: 263-270.

Shen R (2010) World surfactant market. *ACM Intellig.* **1**: 630 p.

Sivapathasekaran C, Mukherjee S, Ray A, Gupta A, Sen R (2010) Artificial neural network modelling and genetic algorithm based medium optimization for the improved production of marine biosurfactant. *Bioresour. Technol.* **101**: 2884-2887.

Riedmiller M, Braun H (1993) A direct adaptive method for faster backpropagation learning: the rprop algorithm. *ICANN* : 586-591.

Rummelhart DE, Hinton GE, Williams RJ (1986) Learning internal representation by error propagation. *Parallel DistributedProcess* . **1**: 318-362.

Setiono R (2001) Feedforward neural network construction using cross validation. *Neural Comput.* **13**(2): 2865-2877.

Thodulur A, Ramirez WF, Mclillan JD (2000) Interpolated parameter functions for neural network models. *Comput. Chem. Eng.* **24**(11): 2545-2553.

Vieira S, Hoffman R (1989) Experimental statistics. *Atlas.*

Zhu CH, Lu FP, He YN, Zhang JK, Du LX (2007) Statistical optimization of medium components for avilamycin production by *streptomyces viridochromogenes* tu57-1 using response surface methodology . *J. Ind. Microbiol. Biotechnol.* **34**(4): 271-278.

Table 1 Levels and values of the independent variables in the 2-factor central composite design

Variable	Level				
	-1,41	-1	0	+ 1	+1,41
Independent					
$(NH_4)_2SO_4$ (% w/v)	0,3975	0,5	0,75	1,0	1,1025
KH_2PO_4 (% w/v)	0,1925	0,5	1,25	2,0	2,3075

Table 2 Factorial planning 23 carried out to investigate the influence of pH and concentrations of

NH4SO4 and KH_2 PO4 on surface tension

Essay	pH	NH4SO4 (%p/v)	KH2PO4 (%p/v)	TS (mN/m)
1	6	0,50	0,50	42,07
2	**14**	**0,50**	**0,50**	**31,72**
3	6	1,50	0,50	35,26
4	**14**	**1,50**	**0,50**	**37,94**
5	6	0,50	1,50	49,39
6	**14**	**0,50**	**1,50**	**33,57**
7	6	1,50	1,50	37,90
8	**14**	**1,50**	**1,50**	**29,89**
9	10	1,00	1,00	36,97
10	10	1,00	1,00	39,08
11	10	1,00	1,00	33,92
12	10	1,00	1,00	42,20

Table 3 Central composite planning 22, carried out as a strategy for optimising the biosurfactant production

process, used to generate the experimental database for modelling the fermentation media.

Essay	NH4SO4 (%p/v)	KH2PO4 (%p/v)	TS (mN/m)
1	0,50	0,50	40,59±1,71
2	1,00	0,50	38,68±2,75
3	0,50	2,00	35,19±0,88
4	1,00	2,00	35,68±1,20
5	**0,40**	**1,25**	**33,85±1,00**
6	1,10	1,25	35,12±1,56
7	0,75	0,19	36,59±4,51
8	0,75	2,31	38,00±0,22
9	0,75	1,25	35,94±3,22
10	0,75	1,25	36,40±1,35
11	0,75	1,25	35,99±1,43

Table 4 Analysis of Variance (ANOVA) for the regression model representing surface tension.

Source of Variation	SQ	GL	SQM	Fcal	Ftab 0.05	Fcal/Ftab	p(F>0.76)
Regression	15,342	5	3,068	0,76	5,05	0,15	0,616
Waste	20,252	5	4,050				
Lack of Adjustment	**20,128**	**3**	**6,709**	**108,56**	**19,16**	**5,66**	**0,0091**
Pure Error	0,124	2	0,062				
Total	35,594	10	3,559				

$R^2 = 0.431$ R=0.656

Table 5 Best performing networks in simulations with the training set

Number of neurons	mse	rmse	R^2	Training algorithm
1	0,3219	0,5674	0,0558	traingda
2	0,1900	0,4359	0,6169	traingda
6	0,0463	0,2152	0,9259	traingda
8	**0,0019**	**0,0436**	**0,9969**	**trainrp**
10	0,0031	0,0557	0,9954	trainrp
15	0,0030	0,0548	0,9962	trainrp
16	0,0073	0,0854	0,9890	traingda

| 20 | 0,0043 | 0,0656 | 0,9930 | traingda |

traingda - backpropagation algorithm with variable learning rate trainrp - resilient backpropagation algorithm

Table 6 Best performing networks in simulations with the validation set

Number of neurons	mse	rmse	R^2	Training algorithm
1	0,1730	0,4159	-0,0375	traingda
2	0,1145	0,3384	0,6191	traingda
6	0,0412	0,2030	0,8835	traingda
8	**0,0015**	**0,0387**	**0,9960**	**trainrp**
10	0,0019	0,0436	0,9944	trainrp
15	0,0017	0,0412	0,9951	trainrp
16	0,0089	0,0943	0,9735	traingda
20	0,0046	0,0678	0,9875	traingda

traingda - backpropagation algorithm with variable learning rate trainrp - resilient backpropagation algorithm

Table 7 Best performing networks in simulations with the test set

Number of neurons	mse	rmse	R^2	Training algorithm
1	0,2325	0,4822	-0,2456	traingda
2	0,1416	0,3763	0,6057	traingda
6	0,0351	0,1873	0,9158	traingda
8	**0,0021**	**0,0458**	**0,9953**	**trainrp**
10	0,0023	0,0480	0,9947	trainrp
15	0,0022	0,0469	0,9954	trainrp
16	0,0058	0,0762	0,9861	traingda
20	0,0037	0,0608	0,9911	traingda

traingda - backpropagation algorithm with variable learning rate trainrp - resilient backpropagation algorithm

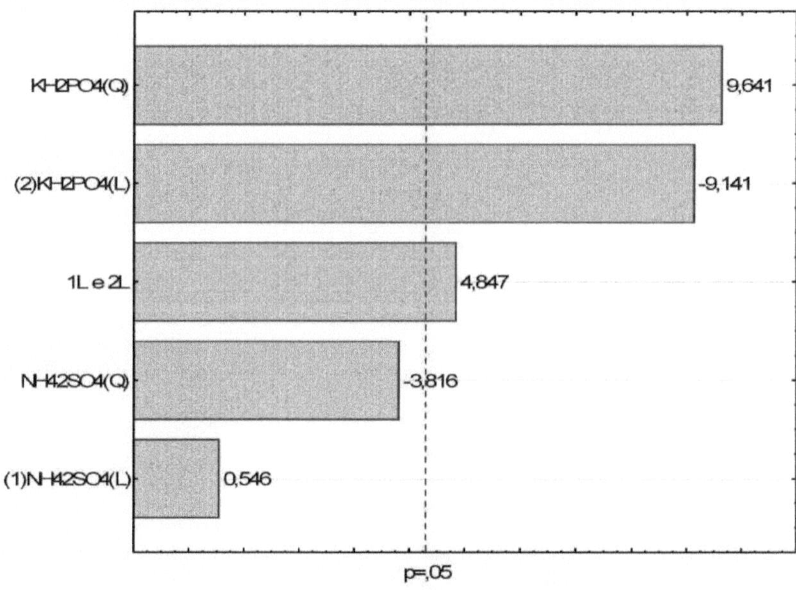

Figura 1 Pareto diagrams for central composite planning, with the independent variables being the concentrations of ammonium sulphate and potassium phosphate and the response variable being the tension of the cell-free culture at 96 hours.

47

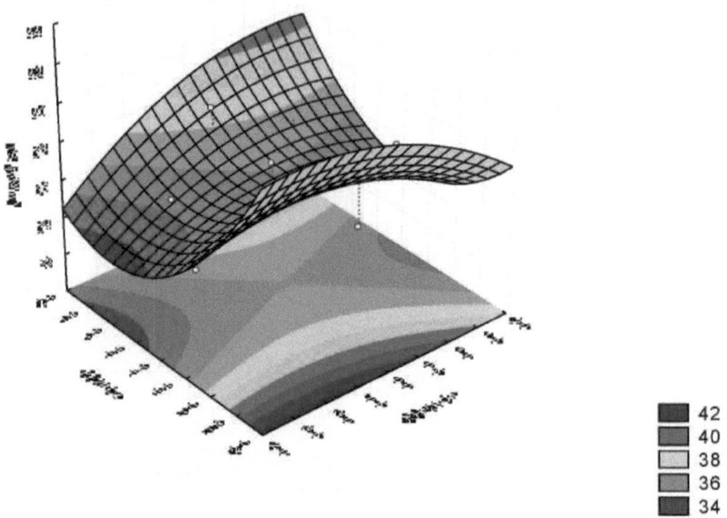

Figura 2   Response surface for surface tension showing the interactions between the concentrations of ammonium sulphate and monobasic potassium phosphate.

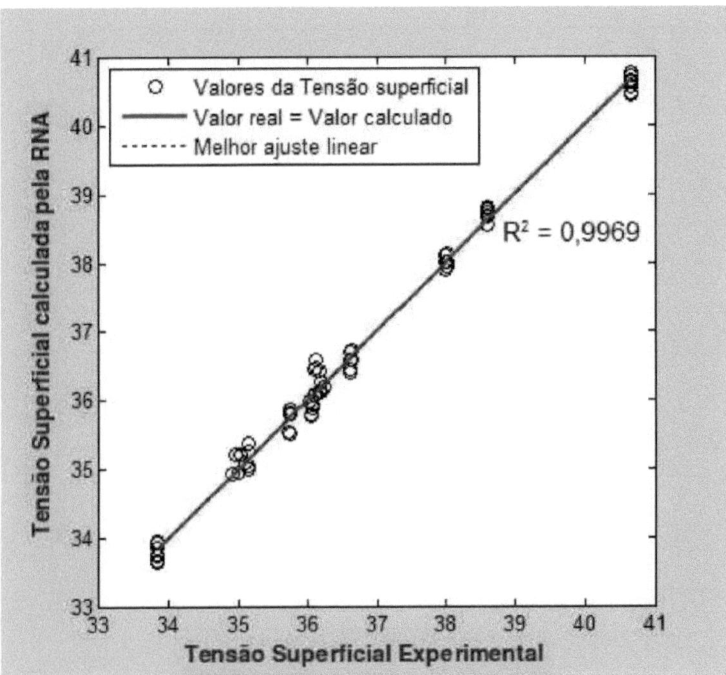

Figura 3 Parity graph between the experimental values from the training set and the values calculated by the network. The circles (○) represent the surface tension values of the experimental values for the training set. The red line (—) represents the best linear fit between the experimental values and those calculated by the network. The dashed line (---) represents the perfect linear fit between the two axes of the graph in the figure. Figure 4 also shows that the linear fit between the experimental and calculated values was practically equal to the perfect linear fit.

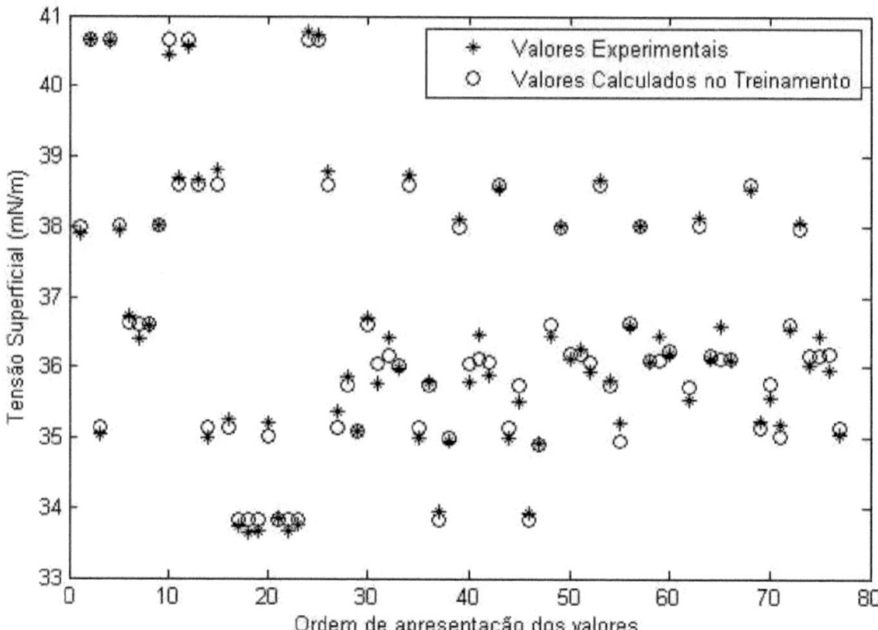

Figura 4   Experimental values from the training set and the values calculated by the artificial neural network during training. The asterisks (*) represent the surface tension values of the experimental values for the training set. The circles (○) represent the values calculated by the network during training, where it can be seen that over 90% of the points coincide.

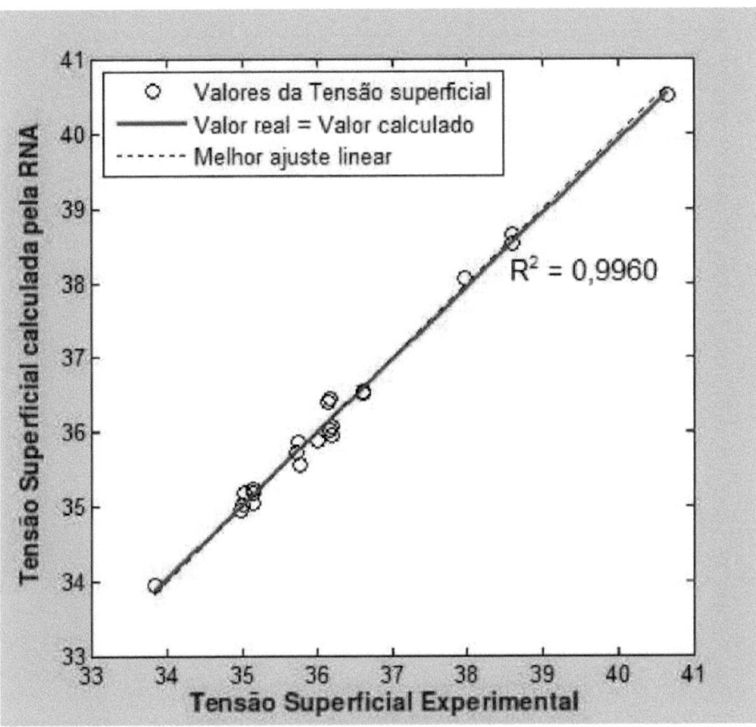

Figura 5 Parity graph between the experimental values from the validation set and the values calculated by the network. The circles (○) represent the surface tension values of the experimental values for the validation set. The red line (—) represents the best linear fit between the experimental values and those calculated by the network. The dashed line (---) represents the perfect linear fit between the two axes of the graph in the figure. Figure 5 also shows that the linear fit between the experimental and calculated values was practically the same as the perfect linear fit.

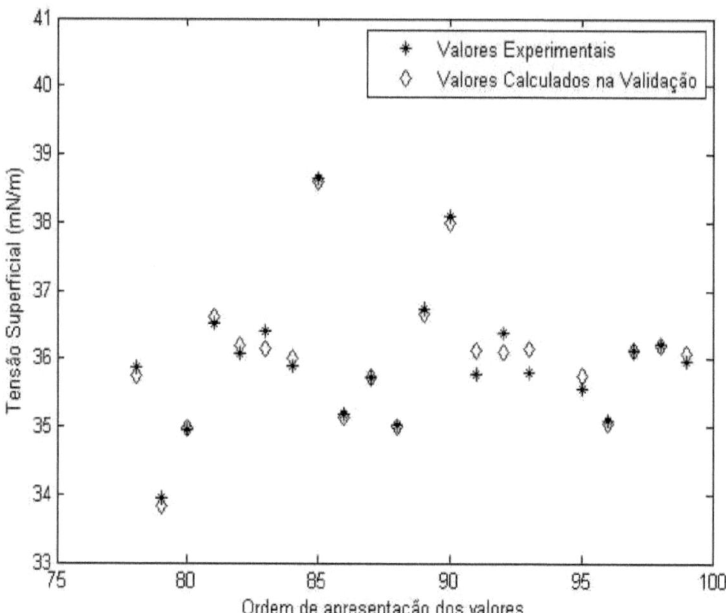

Figura 6 Experimental values from the validation set and the values calculated by the artificial neural network during validation. The asterisks (*) represent the surface tension values of the experimental values for the validation set. The diamonds (◊) represent the values calculated by the network during validation, where it can be seen that more than 80% of the points are coincident.

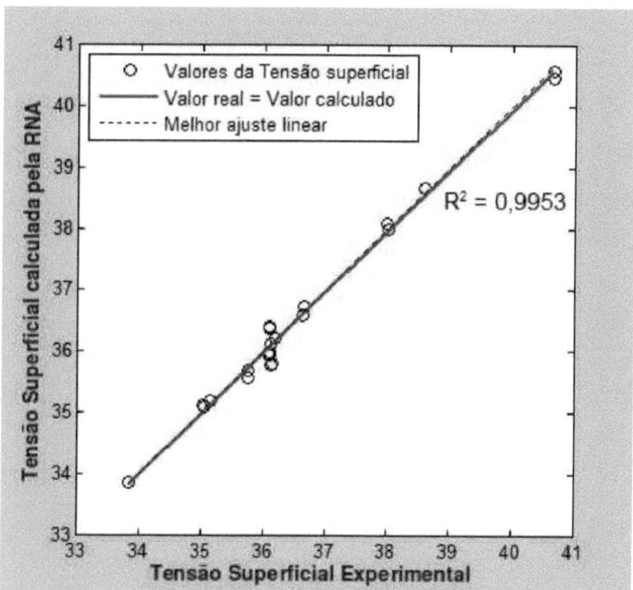

Figura 7   Parity graph between the experimental values of the test set and the values calculated by the network. The circles (o) represent the surface tension values of the experimental values for the test set. The red line (—) represents the best linear fit between the experimental values and those calculated by the network. The dashed line (---) represents the perfect linear fit between the two axes of the graph in the figure. Figure 6 also shows that the linear fit between the experimental and calculated values was practically the same as the perfect linear fit.

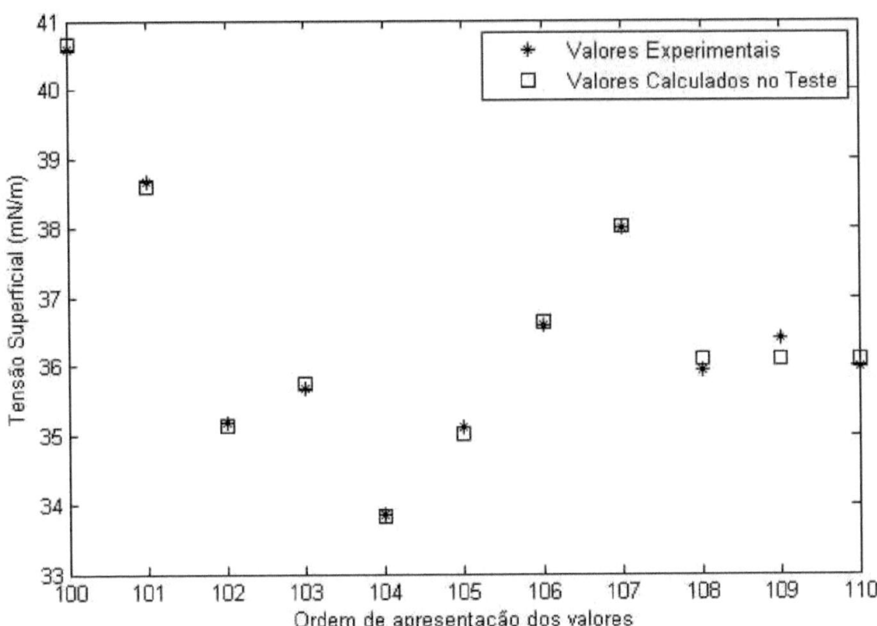

Figura 8   Experimental values of the test set and the values calculated by the artificial neural network during the test. The asterisks (*) represent the surface tension values of the experimental values for the test set. The squares (□) represent the values calculated by the network during the test, where it can be seen that more than 70 per cent of the points coincide.

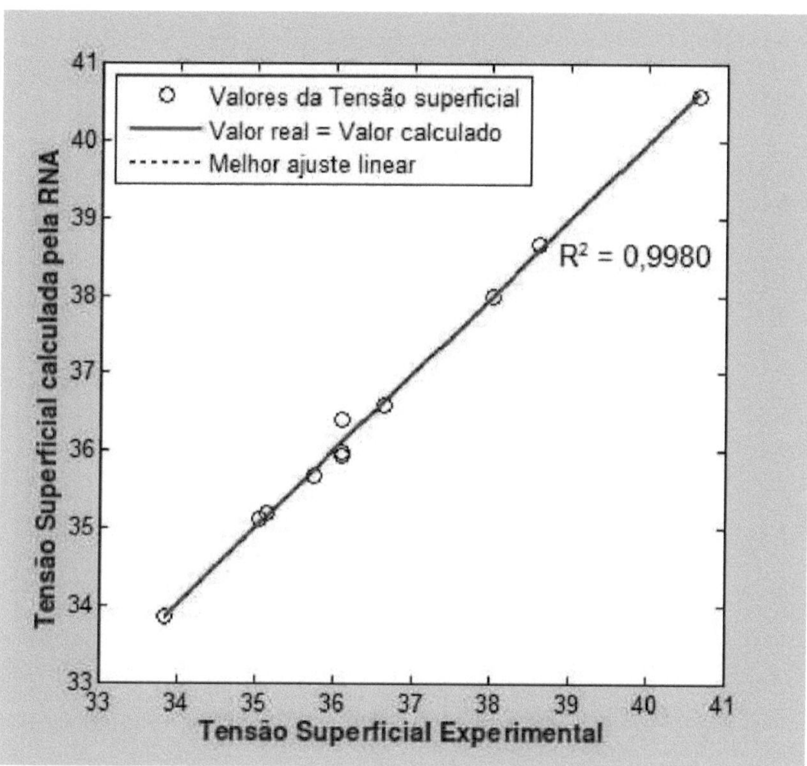

Figura 9 Parity graph between the original experimental values from the central composite planning (Table 3) and the values calculated by the network. The white circles (o) represent the surface tension values of the experimental values, referring to the original set. The red line (—) represents the best linear fit between the experimental values and those calculated by the network. The dashed line (---) represents the perfect linear fit between the two axes of the graph in the figure. Figure 7 also shows that the linear fit between the experimental and calculated values was practically the same as the perfect linear fit.

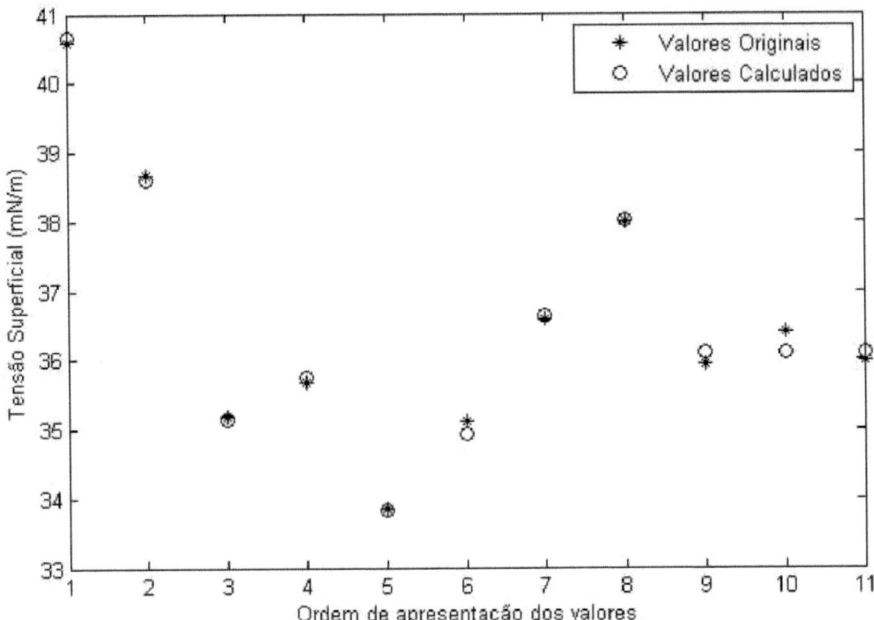

Figure 10 Experimental values from the original set and the values calculated by the artificial neural network for the original input values (Table 3). The asterisks (*) represent the surface tension values of the original experimental values. The circles (○) represent the values calculated by the network with the original values as input, where it can be seen that more than 70% of the points coincide.

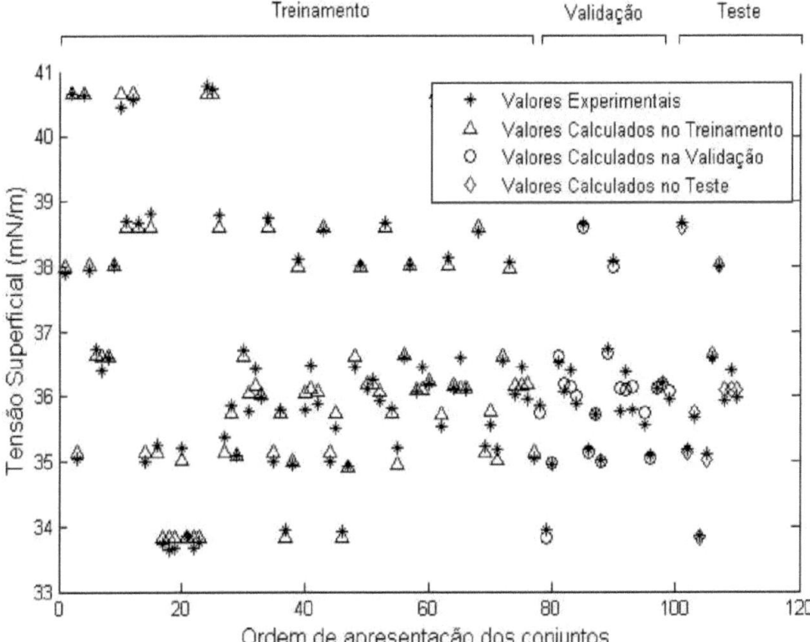

Figure 11 Experimental values from the original set and the values calculated by the artificial neural network for the values in the training, validation and test sets. The asterisks (*) represent the surface tension values of the original experimental values. The triangles (Δ) represent the values calculated by the network with the training values as input, the circles (o) represent the values calculated by the network with the validation values as input and the diamonds (0) represent the values calculated by the network with the test values as input, where it can be seen that over 70% of the points coincide.

yes
I want morebooks!

Buy your books fast and straightforward online - at one of world's fastest growing online book stores! Environmentally sound due to Print-on-Demand technologies.

Buy your books online at
www.morebooks.shop

Kaufen Sie Ihre Bücher schnell und unkompliziert online – auf einer der am schnellsten wachsenden Buchhandelsplattformen weltweit! Dank Print-On-Demand umwelt- und ressourcenschonend produzi ert.

Bücher schneller online kaufen
www.morebooks.shop

info@omniscriptum.com
www.omniscriptum.com

FSC
www.fsc.org
MIX
Papier aus verantwortungsvollen Quellen
Paper from responsible sources
FSC® C105338